$3.$ $\frac{00}{00}$

D1013174

A New Owner's
Guide to
MALTESE

JG-134

Opposite page: Ch. Sand Island Small Kraft Lite, "Henry," is the top-winning Maltese of all time. Owned by Carol F. Andersen, handled by Vicki Abbott.

The Publisher wishes to acknowledge the following owners of the dogs in this book: Vicki and Larry Abbott, Carol F. Andersen, Debbie Burke, Emanuel Cominiti, Vivianne Creelman, Kathy DiGiacomo, Lucille M. Dillon, Gay Glazbrook, Karen S. Grace, Eleanor Grassick, Mamie R. Gregory, Claudia Grunstra, Lee Guzman, Arlene M. Johnson, Joseph F. Joly III, Sandra Kenner, Debbie Kirsch, Robin Lindemann, Sharon and David Newcomb, Andrea Nöel, Chris Pearson, Connie Phillips, Julie Phillips, Bonnie Puia, Beverly Quilliam, Rosemarie Saccardi, Mariko Sukezaki, Christopher Vicari, Roberta Werner, Dorothy White.

Photographers: Alverson Photographers, John Ashbey, Booth Photography, Paulette Braun, Callea Photography, Isabelle Francais, Michele Perlmutter, Don Petrulis, Evelyn Shafer, Alex Smith, Perry Struse, Taylor Taylor, Missy Yuhl.

Distributed in the UNITED STATES to the Pet Trade by T.F.H. Publications, Inc., One T.F.H. Plaza, Neptune City, NJ 07753; distributed in the UNITED STATES to the Bookstore and Library Trade by National Book Network, Inc. 4720 Boston Way, Lanham MD 20706; in CANADA to the Pet Trade by H & L Pet Supplies Inc., 27 Kingston Crescent, Kitchener, Ontario N2B 2T6; Rolf C. Hagen Inc., 3225 Sartelon St. Laurent-Montreal Quebec H4R 1E8; in CANADA to the Book Trade by Vanwell Publishing Ltd., 1 Northrup Crescent, St. Catharines, Ontario L2M 6P5 ; in ENGLAND by T.F.H. Publications, PO Box 15, Waterlooville PO7 6BQ; in AUSTRALIA AND THE SOUTH PACIFIC by T.F.H. (Australia), Pty. Ltd., Box 149, Brookvale 2100 N.S.W., Australia; in NEW ZEALAND by Brooklands Aquarium Ltd. 5 McGiven Drive, New Plymouth, RD1 New Zealand; in Japan by T.F.H. Publications, Japan—Jiro Tsuda, 10-12-3 Ohjidai, Sakura, Chiba 285, Japan; in SOUTH AFRICA by Lopis (Pty) Ltd., P.O. Box 39127, Booysens, 2016, Johannesburg, South Africa. Published by T.F.H. Publications, Inc.
MANUFACTURED IN THE
UNITED STATES OF AMERICA
BY T.F.H. PUBLICATIONS, INC.

A NEW OWNER'S GUIDE TO
MALTESE

VICKI ABBOTT

Contents

1997 Edition

The Maltese's happy nature shows in his expression.

A job well done deserves a reward.

The Maltese is a lot of personality in a little package.

The Maltese's flowing white coat is the breed's trademark.

It's nice to have friends to snuggle with!

DEDICATION

To my husband Larry, whose total support has been the foundation for my success, and to Tara and Aubrey, who have not only been delightful daughters but also an invaluable part of the Scylla Maltese team. And to our friend Jere Olson, without whom there never would have existed a little dog called "Henry"–the top-winning Maltese of all time.

"Henry" has earned the distinction of Greatest Winning Maltese and Top winning Toy Dog of All Time, according to Kennel Review *magazine statistics.*

Larry and Vicki Abbott with Ch. Shanlyn's Rais'n A Raucous, "Scrapper."

HISTORY of the Maltese

ogs of all breeds, from the tiniest Maltese to the largest Great Dane, have one thing in common. They can all trace their ancestry back through the ages to a common ancestor. As inconceivable as it may seem when we look at our Maltese and compare it to a Bulldog or perhaps a Greyhound, that ancestor is none other than the one known today as *Canis lupus*—the wolf!

Just when the wolf came in out of the forest and took up residence with its human counterparts is a matter of conjecture. However, most research determines that it was some time during the Mesolithic period, which was over ten thousand years ago. As these wolves became increasingly more domesticated, man undoubtedly realized he could direct their abilities to advantageously assist him in hunting and other survival pursuits.

With the passing of time, humans also began to see they could manipulate breedings of these *wolves-cum-dogs* so that the resulting offspring were extremely proficient in particular areas. As human populations developed a more sophisticated lifestyle, their needs became far more diversified. Customizing the evolving wolves to suit these growing human needs was inevitable. The wolves became hunters, guardians and stock drovers. The manner in which these companions to man became useful was as diverse as the human population itself .

As human settlements and encampments developed into towns and villages, life became easier and mankind found time

All breeds of dog, even those as tiny as the Maltese, share the wolf as a common ancestor.

8

Through selective breeding, different types of dogs came to have different duties. Some breeds, like the Maltese, had the sole purpose of being companion dogs.

that could be devoted to pursuits other than simply staying alive. By this time, through selective breeding, man's personal wolves had evolved into a species so different they could be classified as *Canis familiaris* — domestic dog. Eventually, some of the dogs were kept with no duties other than to be companions or, perhaps, to provide an occasional warning bark when they suspected the invasion of their household by an intruder.

There is documentation of controlled breeding practices by the Romans occurring as early as the first century A.D. The Romans had categorized the many types of dogs into six general classifications. These categories are strikingly similar to the "variety groups" used as a classification method by the American

As a pup, this Bichon Frise bears a striking resemblance to his Maltese "cousins." Both breeds are known for their all-white coats.

Kennel Club today. Roman writers talked of "house guardian dogs, shepherd dogs, sporting dogs, war dogs, scent dogs and sight dogs" two thousand years ago. Many of today's breeds can trace their ancestry directly back to breeds that were included in those early groups.

Through the ages, most wolves and wild dogs were large and dark in color. Man's sophistication brought a desire for something "different." Humans developed an admiration for smaller light-colored dogs. Dogs that once were primarily under the jurisdiction of the male population were moving into homes and becoming the property of women as well, and as cities developed, space constraints made it increasingly more difficult to house large dogs. Those who required the companionship of a dog found need for animals demanding less space. Thus, small dogs became very popular, and in many households became members of the family.

Companion and toy breeds are known to have existed even before dynastic times in Egypt. Pictures of very small, lightly colored dogs with silken coats appear on urns and vases excavated from the ruins of ancient Greece. These are thought to be descendants of more wolf-like dogs resembling today's spitz-type dogs.

As far back as 600 to 300 B.C. there is documentation that a family of generally white, small "lap" or ladies' dogs existed throughout the Mediterranean area. Several breeds of dog are known to have descended from this origin, including the Poodle, the Maltese and four "varieties" or subgroups of the Bichon. While each of the breeds descended from these originating small white dogs lay claim as the "source" of the others, in truth all are descended from the same root stock. They are all "cousins" rather than any one being a direct descendent of the other.

Poodles share the Maltese's origin as lap dogs in the Mediterranean region. Poodles, however, are seen in three different sizes and a variety of colors.

THE MALTESE AS A BREED

Historical reference to the Maltese breed is made under the names Bichon Maltaise, Melitei, Melita and Maltese. The name Bichon Maltaise can be explained by the fact that a now extinct variety of the Bichon was once known by that name. Whether this was a forerunner of today's Maltese appears to be highly unlikely. The Carthaginians referred to Malta as Melita and Melitei simply means having come from Malta.

While the existence of the Maltese as such can not be pinpointed to a precise point in time, it is certain this type of small white lap dog existed on the little island of Malta as far back as the days of ancient Greece. Malta is located in the middle of the Mediterranean Sea. The entire island occupies only 150 or so square miles, but while small, its location is strategic. It lies almost midway between Africa and Europe and less than 75 miles from Sicily, which is a stepping stone to Italy through which the entire European continent is easily reached.

With total area so highly restricted, it is obvious that space for housing dogs would be at a high premium. If the inhabitants of Malta were to keep dogs at all, good sense would clearly dictate they could not be large—in fact, the smaller the better. Confined to the island, bloodlines were naturally restricted and while in many respects unintentional, a controlled program developed so that a very distinctive little white dog emerged that became known as the Maltese. In addition to being highly attractive, the breed was clever, easily trained and entirely devoted to its owners.

Malta's strategic location led to its development as an important trading center. As goods moved eastward to the exotic Orient by caravan and westward through sea routes, the little white dogs traveled along with their owners. Their unique size, beauty and pleasant natures led them to become items of barter and gifts to royalty. The little dogs are known to have influenced the many breeds indigenous to these new lands.

The Maltese in Great Britain

To illustrate the extent to which the Maltese traveled, and to which it was highly esteemed, in the late 1500s England's Queen Elizabeth was given a Maltese as a gift that had been bred in Turkey! The British dog fancy took the breed both to its heart and to its bed. Dog writers extolled the virtues of the little breed, not the least of which were medicinal powers.

It was not uncommon at that time to believe the toy breeds could draw rheumatic pains from their owners. The little dogs were put under the bed covers at their owners' feet in hopes of relieving the pain that accompanied the rheumatoid condition. Among the many nicknames given the breed was "comforter," not only because of the breed's loving and devoted nature but because of the belief that it was capable of reducing pain in the joints of the owner.

In the descriptions of the breed through the centuries, several things remained constant: the white silken coat, the diminutive size and the loving but stalwart nature. Though small, it is obvious the Maltese's brave nature can be traced back through antiquity.

Popularity of the breed was to rise and fall as centuries passed in England, so much so that in 1888 the famed dog writer "Stonehenge" was to write of the breed in *The Dogs of Great Britain , America and Other Countries as:* ". . .so scarce some time ago, as to induce Sir E. Landseer to paint one as the last of his race; since which several have been imported from Malta and, though still scarce, they are now to be obtained." Stonehenge went on to say of the breed: "This beautiful little dog is a Skye Terrier in miniature, with, however, a far more silky coat, a considerably shorter back and tail stiffly curved over the hip." He cautioned, "The weight should never exceed 5 or 6 pounds" and described the long hair as being particularly "transparent and silky." He extolled the nature of the breed and predicted its resurgence as a popular household pet.

Stonehenge discusses a strain of Maltese bred by a Mr. Mandeville which he says "kept possession of the show bench since 1862 when the first class of this kind of toy dog was established at the Agricultural Hall Show (in London)." Interest continued on at a modest rate in England and by the turn of the century the Maltese had achieved its

Peggy Hogg handles Ch. Joanne Chen's Maya Dancer, a top-winning Maltese of the early 1970s, to a Best in Show win. Owned by Mamie R. Gregory.

greatest level of popularity. During this period, a good many of the breed were exported to the United States and Canada where the breed was enjoying even greater acceptance and popularity.

THE MALTESE IN AMERICA

The first Maltese registered by the American Kennel Club were entered in the Stud Book in 1888. They were the bitches "Snips" and "Topsy," neither of which boasted a pedigree. The numbers grew very slowly but steadily so that by 1950 just over 70 Maltese had been registered with the AKC.

Ch. Pendleton's Jewel was a top winner in the late 1960s and early 1970s. Bred by Anne Pendleton, owned by Dorothy White.

The breed's popularity increased dramatically at this point. In 1970, over 4,000 Maltese were registered, and every year since the breed's popularity has increased among breeders, fanciers and pet owners.

The first Maltese champion recorded by the AKC was Mrs. C.S. Young's Thackery Rob Roy, whelped in 1901. The first American all breed Best in Show was won by Mrs. Carl Baumann's Ch. Sweetsir of Dyker born in 1912.

In the 1940s, Dr. Vincenzo Calvaresi came upon the Maltese scene. His breeding program produced over one hundred champions. Far more important than the number of quality champions produced under his Villa Malta prefix, however, was the doctor's great sense of showmanship and flair for the dramatic. The attention of fanciers of all breeds was focused on the many beautiful and strikingly identical braces and teams he campaigned from coast to coast.

There can be little doubt that Tony and Aennchen Antonelli did more to popularize the Maltese as a show dog and companion than any fancier that may have preceded them. The Antonellis began breeding in the 1950s and, though breeding ceased with the death of Aennchen in 1975, the names of their record-shattering winners and producers stand as icons in the Maltese world to this day. In addition to their unparalleled contribution by way of great producers and winners, the Antonellis are credited for bringing about the establishment of the breed's parent club, the American Maltese Association. It was through their efforts that the many independently operated Maltese organizations were united on December 3, 1961.

STANDARD for the Maltese

The American Kennel Club standard for the Maltese is written in simple, straightforward language that can be read and understood by even the beginning fancier. However, its implications take many years to fully understand. This can only be accomplished through observing many quality Maltese over the years and reading as much about the breed as possible. There are some breeds that change drastically from puppyhood to adulthood. It would be extremely difficult for the untrained eye to determine the actual breed of some purebred dogs in puppyhood. This is not quite so with the Maltese outside of the length of the mature dog's coat. In fact, at eight weeks of age, a Maltese puppy will reflect in miniature what it will look like in many respects at maturity.

It must be remembered that a breed standard describes the "perfect" Maltese, but no dog is perfect and no Maltese, not even the greatest dog show winner, will possess every quality asked for in its perfect form. It is how closely an individual dog adheres to the standard of the breed that determines its show potential.

One of the obvious things that make the Maltese such an attractive dog is its beautiful white silky coat and contrasting black "points" (eyes, nose and lips). A good part of the breed's

Sand Island Northern Lites's show potential was evident even as a young pup. Pictured here at four months old, she went on to become a Group winner.

appeal also comes from the fearless and dynamic temperament. While gentle, the breed is lively and playful, and one look into the sparkling black eyes of the Maltese tells you the breed is also capable of being entirely mischievous.

Size is very important to the breed as the Maltese is a toy breed—a lap dog. The ideal Maltese is always under seven pounds in weight.

In addition the Maltese is beautifully balanced. Though small, it is never ungainly or clumsy appearing.

As a toy breed, size is a very important aspect of the Maltese's conformation. The dog's body should be compact and should create an overall impression of elegance.

Henry is the picture of what a Maltese should look like—small and elegant, with the beautiful flowing coat that is the breed's trademark.

The body is compact with sufficient length of neck to keep the overall picture one of elegance and agility.

Just because it is a toy breed, there

is no reason for the Maltese to be unsound. The standard's requirements for construction reveal well-made limbs and an easy way of moving. The breed's balanced construction permits graceful easy movement. Since the breed standard describes very normal construction and does not call for any unusual features of construction, there should be no physical abnormalities.

OFFICIAL STANDARD

The following is the official standard for the Maltese, as adopted by the American Maltese Association and approved March 10, 1964:

General Appearance—The Maltese is a toy dog covered from head to foot with a mantle of long, silky, white hair. He is gentle-mannered and affectionate, eager and sprightly in action, and, despite his size, possesssed of the vigor needed for the satisfactory companion.

Head—Of medium length and in proportion to the size of the dog. The skull is slightly rounded on top, the stop moderate. The drop ears are rather low set and heavily feathered with long hair that hangs close to the head. Eyes are set not too far apart; they are very dark and round, their black rims enhancing the gentle yet alert expression. The muzzle is of medium length, fine and tapered but not snipy. The nose is black. The teeth meet in an even, edge-to-edge bite, or in a scissors bite.

Neck—Sufficient length of neck is desirable as promoting a high carriage of the head.

Body—Compact, the height from the withers to the ground equaling the length from the withers to the root of the tail. Shoulder blades are sloping, the elbows well knit and held

The Maltese's dark eyes, nose, and mouth are a contrast to his silky white coat. The expression should be alert, yet gentle, and should accent the dog's overall appearance.

close to the body. The back is level in topline, the ribs well sprung. The chest is fairly deep, the loins taut, strong, and just slightly tucked up underneath.

Tail–A long-haired plume carried gracefully over the back, its tip lying to the side over the quarter.

Legs and Feet–Legs are fine-boned and nicely feathered. Forelegs are straight, their pastern joints well knit and devoid of appreciable bend. Hind legs are strong and moderately angulated at stifles and hocks.

The Maltese embodies grace in every feature, from top knot to tail. His tail should be carried over his back with the tip lying to one side.

The feet are small and round, with toe pads black. Scraggly hairs on the feet may be trimmed to give a neater appearance.

Coat and Color–The coat is single, that is, without undercoat. It hangs long, flat and silky over the sides of the body almost, if not quite, to the ground. The long head-hair may be tied up in a topknot or it may be left hanging. Any suggestion of kinkiness, curliness, or woolly texture is objectionable. Color, pure white. Light tan or lemon on the ears is permissible, but not desirable.

Size–Weight under 7 pounds, with from 4 to 6 pounds preferred. Over-all quality is to be favored over size.

Gait–The Maltese moves with a jaunty, smooth, flowing gait. Viewed from the side, he gives an impression of rapid movement, size considered. In the stride, the forelegs reach straight and free from the shoulders, with elbows close. Hind legs to move in a straight line. Cowhocks or any suggestion of hind leg toeing in or out are faults.

Temperament–For all his diminutive size, the Maltese seems to be without fear. His trust and affectionate responsiveness are very appealing. He is among the gentlest mannered of all little dogs, yet he is lively and playful as well as vigorous.

CHARACTERISTICS of the Maltese

Before anyone tries to decide whether or not the Maltese is the correct breed for them, a larger more important question must be asked: "Should I own a dog at all?" Dog ownership is a serious and time-consuming responsibility that should not be entered into lightly. Failure to understand this can make what should be a rewarding relationship instead one of sheer drudgery. It is also one of the primary reasons for thousands upon thousands of unwanted dogs' lives ending in the gas chambers of humane societies and animal shelters throughout America.

If the prospective dog owner lives alone and conditions are conducive to dog ownership, all he or she need do is be sure that there is a strong desire to make the necessary commitment dog ownership entails. In the case of family households, the situation is a much more complicated one. It is vital that the person who will actually be responsible for the dog's care really wants a dog. In many households, mothers are most often given the additional responsibility of caring for the family pets. Children are away at school all day. Father is at work. Often it is the mother who is saddled with the additional chores of housebreaking, feeding and trips to the veterinary hospital with what was supposed to be a family project.

Learn all you can about dog ownership and the specific traits of the Maltese before you decide to bring one into your life.

Nearly all children love puppies and dogs and will promise anything to get one. But childhood enthusiasm can wane very

The Maltese is a toy breed, but they can't be treated like toys. Baby Twinkle is an adorable pup, but she's also a living, breathing animal who needs love and care.

quickly and it will be up to the adults in the family to ensure the dog receives proper care. Children should be taught responsibility, but to expect a living, breathing and needy animal to teach a child this lesson is incredibly indifferent to the needs of the animal.

There are also many households in which the entire family is gone from early morning until late in the day. The question that must be asked then is who will provide food for the dog and access to the out-of-doors if the dog is expected not to relieve itself in the house? This is something that can probably be worked out with an adult dog but it is totally unfair for anyone to expect a young puppy to be left alone the entire day.

Should an individual or family find they are capable of providing the proper home for a dog or young puppy, suitability of breed must also be considered. Here it might be worthwhile to look at the difference between owning a purebred dog and one of mixed ancestry

THE CASE FOR THE PUREBRED DOG

A mongrel can give you as much love and devotion as a purebred dog. However, the manner in which the dog does this and how its personality, energy level and the amount of care it requires suit an individual's lifestyle are major considerations. In a purebred dog, most of these considerations are predictable to a marked degree even if the dog is purchased as a very young puppy. A puppy of uncertain parentage will not give you this assurance.

Although every dog has a unique individual personality, a purebred Maltese's temperament will be predictable to a certain degree.

All puppies are cute and fairly manageable but someone who lives in a two-room apartment will find life difficult with a dog that grows to the size of a Great Dane. The mountain climber or marathon runner is not going to be happy with a short-nosed breed that has difficulty catching its breath simply walking across the street on a hot summer day.

An owner who expects his dog to sit quietly by his side while its master watches television or reads is not going to be particularly happy with a high-strung off-the-wall dog whose rest requirements are only 30 seconds out of every 10 hours! The outdoorsman is not going to be particularly happy with a long-coated breed that attracts every burr, leaf and insect in all of nature.

Knowing what kind of dog best suits your lifestyle is not just a consideration, it is paramount to the foundation of your life-long relationship with the dog. If the dog you are considering does not fit your lifestyle, the relationship simply will not last.

LIFE WITH A MALTESE

All of the foregoing applies to whether or not you should own a Maltese. Further, as greeting-card appealing as an adorable Maltese puppy might be, remember it is a white long-coated dog that needs a great deal of care! Daily brushing and frequent bathing is a must. When the Maltese is outdoors it is no less a dog than any other. It enjoys playing in the mud, burying itself in the sandbox or rolling in the brambles as

much as a dog of any other breed would. This must be dealt with immediately.

The Maltese is a long-coated breed that will only stay healthy and looking like a Maltese as long as you are willing to invest the time in keeping it that way. If you do not feel you have the time to do this yourself, it will be necessary to have a professional groomer do this for you. If you appreciate the look of the breed, realize it will take more than a little effort on your part to keep it looking that way.

The Maltese is noted for its long, silky, white hair, which is referred to as a "single coat." This means that, like human hair, it has no soft, downy undercoat. This can prove to be a boon to individuals allergic to dogs or dog hair. They will either not be allergic to Maltese or the reaction will, in many cases, be significantly less. However, like many all-white and pink-skinned dogs, the breed can be extremely sensitive to fleas. Unless carefully controlled, flea bites can and will lead to severe scratching

The Maltese's classic beauty gives it that "greeting card" appeal, but Maltese are more than just pretty faces. In fact, they can be just as mischievous as any breed!

When properly introduced, the easygoing Maltese can peacefully co-exist with other dogs and household pets. Scrapper poses with his Australian Shepherd friend.

that results in skin eruptions and "hot spots," which are accompanied by hair loss.

If you are willing to make the necessary commitment that a Maltese requires, let us assure you there are few breeds that are any more versatile, amiable and adaptable. While the Maltese may well have been the pampered pet of Madame and spent the night tucked under the covers of her bed, don't forget the Maltese was a seafarer and a member of desert caravans. It also was practically an endangered species at one time. A dog cannot endure conditions of this nature without a strong constitution. With a history of this kind, it should go without saying that the breed can fit into most loving and caring households.

The breed is a hardy one and if bred by a responsible breeder is seldom prone to chronic illnesses. The Maltese is of a diminutive size but that does not mean it must be treated as if made of egg shells. For its size, the breed has amazing energy and great strength. With proper instruction, children old enough to understand how to handle a small dog can learn to enjoy the exuberant personality of the Maltese and the Maltese in turn will love the gentle children.

The breed is extremely playful and inquisitive. It is one that never ceases to have something to do. Yet a Maltese is just as content to sit by your side when you read or listen to music. Introduced early enough and properly supervised, the Maltese can co-exist with your cat, rabbit or even larger dog as well as it can with humans. The Maltese is a breed of which it can be said without hesitation that two dogs are just as easy to raise as one.

MALE OR FEMALE?

While the sex of a dog in many breeds is a very important consideration, this is not particularly the case with the Maltese. The male Maltese makes just as loving, devoted and trainable a companion as the female. In fact, there are some who believe a male can be even more devoted to his master than a female.

There is one important point to consider in determining your choice between male and female. While both must be trained not to relieve themselves just anywhere in the home, males have a natural instinct to lift their legs and urinate to "mark" their home territory. It seems confusing to many dog owners, but a male's marking of his home turf has absolutely nothing to do with whether or not it is housebroken. The two responses come from entirely different needs and must be dealt with in that manner. Some dogs are more difficult to train not to mark within the confines of the household than others. Males that are used for breeding are even more prone to this response and are even harder to break of doing so.

On the other hand, females have their semiannual "heat" cycles once they have reached sexual maturity. In the case of the female Maltese, this can occur for the first time at about nine or ten months of age. These cycles are accompanied by a vaginal discharge that creates the need to confine the female for about three weeks so that she does not soil her surroundings. It must be understood the female has no control over this bloody discharge so it has nothing to do with training.

While most Maltese are not normally left outdoors by themselves for long stretches of time, this is one time a female should not be outdoors by herself for even a brief moment or two. The need for confinement and keeping a careful watch over the female in heat is especially important to prevent her from becoming pregnant by some neighborhood Lothario. Equally dangerous to her well-being is the male that is much larger than her. The dog may be too large to actually breed her but he could seriously injure or even kill her in his attempts to do so.

Both of these sexually related problems can be entirely eliminated by spaying the female and neutering the male. Unless a Maltese has been purchased expressly for breeding or showing from a breeder capable of making this judgment, the dog should be sexually altered.

Breeding and raising puppies should be left in the hands of people who have the facilities to keep each and every puppy they breed until the correct homes are found for them. This can often take many months after a litter is born. Most single dog owners are not equipped to do this. Naturally, a responsible Maltese owner would never allow his or her pet to roam the streets and end its life in an

The playful Maltese always finds a way to entertain himself and amuse his family. Tyler is owned by Vicki and Larry Abbott and Joseph F. Joly, III.

animal shelter. Unfortunately, being forced to place a puppy due to space constraints before you are able to thoroughly check out the prospective buyer may in fact create this exact situation.

Many times we have had parents ask to buy a female "just as a pet" but with full intentions of breeding so that their children can witness "the birth process." There are countless books and videos now available that portray this wonderful event and do not add to the worldwide pet overpopulation we now face. Altering one's companion dogs not only precludes the possibility of adding to this problem, it also eliminates bothersome household problems and precautions.

It should be understood, however, that spaying and neutering are not reversible procedures. Spayed females or neutered males are not allowed to be shown in American Kennel Club shows, nor will altered animals ever be able to be used for breeding.

THE MALTESE PERSONALITY

Historically, the Maltese has been a close companion to man. Whether darling of the royal courts or international traveler, everything the Maltese has done it has done in the company of humans. It is happiest when allowed to continue that association. It simply would not do for a Maltese to be shut away in a kennel or run with only occasional access to your life and environment. Should this be your intent, you would best be better served by another breed. The very essence of the Maltese is in its unique personality and sensitive and loving nature, which is best developed by constant human contact.

The Maltese is not just a lap dog— Willy is trained to help the hearing impaired. He is a constant companion and "hearing aid" to his owner, Rosemarie Saccardi.

Although the Maltese is certainly not a vindictive breed, we are never surprised to hear that a Maltese that has been completely housebroken will suddenly forget all its manners in protest of suddenly being left alone too often or too long. Some Maltese will let you know they are not getting the attention they need by destroying household items, particularly those things which belong to the individuals the dogs are particularly devoted to and who they are missing.

Vicki Abbott is completely devoted to all of her Maltese, and eight-week-old "Hank" is equally devoted to her.

None of this should be construed to mean that only people who are home all day to cater to every whim of their dogs can be Maltese owners. We know many working people who are away most of the day whose Maltese are well mannered and trustworthy when left home alone. The key here seems to be the quality rather than quantity of time spent with their pets. Morning or evening walks, grooming sessions, game time and simply having your Maltese share your life when you are home is vital to the breed's personality development and attitude. A Maltese likes to be talked to and praised. Like the old adage "no man is an island," this applies to dogs as well, particularly so in the case of the Maltese.

Everything about the Maltese personality indicates it is a non-aggressive breed but that does not mean the breed is shy or withdrawn. On the contrary, the Maltese could well be considered the "welcome wagon" of the canine world! The Maltese insists there will be no strangers in its life, giving special attention to those people who live an entire lifetime saying, "I don't like dogs!" That may well apply to other dogs, but they readily learn the feeling does not apply to the Maltese—at least not for very long!

We have never seen a Maltese even indicate it would challenge its owner on any point regardless of how much it might object to what it is being asked to do. Therefore a stern and disapproving voice is usually more than sufficient to let your Maltese know you disapprove of what it is doing. It is

never necessary to strike a Maltese in any circumstance. A sharp "no" is normally more than it takes to make your point.

Because of its easy-going nature, the Maltese is quite content to remain at home with its family and is not a breed prone to wander off even if it were allowed to do so. But since it is a lover of all humans, a Maltese is not beyond accepting a ride in an automobile or an invitation to play, even if the invitation might come from a total stranger.

Within the confines of its own household, however, the Maltese is an excellent watchdog in the sense that it will sound the alarm if it sees or hears anything unusual. Expect your Maltese to let you know the doorbell has rung or someone is knocking at the door. On the other hand, you will not be disturbed by constant and needless barking.

The inquisitive Maltese wants to be a part of everything that goes on in his home.

The Maltese makes a great effort to please its owner and is highly trainable as long as the trainer is not heavy handed. Training problems encountered are far more apt to be due to the owner rather than to the Maltese not understanding what is to be learned. Although many Maltese owners are inclined to think of their companions as "little people," it must be understood that the Maltese is first and foremost a dog. Dogs, like the wolves from which they are descended, are pack animals and they need a "pack leader." Dogs are now totally dependent upon humans to provide that leadership. When that leadership is not provided, a dog can easily become confused and neurotic.

Setting boundaries is important to the well-being of your Maltese and your relationship to it. The sooner your dog understands there are rules that must be obeyed, the easier it will be for it to become an enjoyable companion. How soon you learn to establish and enforce those rules will determine how quickly this will come about. As you know, the Maltese is not vindictive or particularly stubborn but it does need guidance in order to achieve its potential.

The Maltese makes a great pet for families with children, as long as they are always supervised when together and the children are taught to handle the dog with care.

SELECTING the Maltese for You

The Maltese you buy will live with you for many years to come. It is not the least bit unusual for the well-bred Maltese to live as long as 10, 12, or even 14 or 15 years. Obviously it is important that the Maltese you select has the advantage of beginning life in a healthy environment and comes from sound, healthy stock.

The governing kennel clubs in the different countries of the world maintain lists of local breed clubs and breeders who can lead a prospective Maltese buyer to responsible breeders of quality stock. If you are not sure of where to contact an established Maltese breeder in your area, we strongly

Henry models the impeccably groomed coat that has helped him earn fame in the show ring. Many owners of pet Maltese also put in the effort to maintain their dogs' full coats.

recommend contacting your kennel club for recommendations.

It is very likely that you will be able to find an established Maltese breeder in your own area. If so, you will be able to visit the breeder, inspect the premises and, in many cases, you will also be able to see a puppy's parents and other relatives. These breeders are always willing and able to discuss any problems that might exist in the breed and how they should be dealt with.

Should there be no breeders in your immediate area you can arrange to have a puppy shipped to you. There are breeders throughout the country who have shipped puppies to satisfied owners out of state and even to other countries.

Never hesitate to ask the breeder you visit or deal with any questions or concerns you might have relative to owning a Maltese. You should expect the breeder to ask you a good number of questions as well. Good breeders are just as interested in placing their puppies in a loving and safe environment as you are in obtaining a happy, healthy puppy.

This six-and-a-half-week old pup is too young to leave the breeder. Pups are weaned by eight weeks, but breeders often keep their pups a few weeks after weaning.

A good Maltese breeder will want to know if there are young children in the family and what their ages are. They will also want to know if you or your children have ever owned a dog before. The breeder will want to know if you live in an apartment or in a home. If in a home, they will want to know if you have a fenced yard and if there will be someone home during the day to attend to a young puppy's needs.

Not all good breeders maintain large kennels. In fact, you are more apt to find Maltese come from the homes of small hobby breeders who only keep a few dogs and have litters only occasionally. The names of these people are just as likely to appear on the recommended lists from kennel clubs as the larger kennels that maintain many dogs. Hobby breeders are equally dedicated to breeding quality Maltese and have the distinct advantage of being able to raise their puppies in the

Nursing pups have immunity from infectious diseases; however, they become highly susceptible once weaned. Puppies need to be kept up-to-date on all vaccinations.

home environment with all the accompanying personal attention and socialization.

Again, it is important that both the buyer and the seller ask questions. We would be highly suspect of a person who is willing to sell you a Maltese puppy with no questions asked.

RECOGNIZING A HEALTHY PUPPY

Most Maltese breeders are apt to keep their puppies until they are 12 to 16 weeks of age and have been given all of their puppy inoculations. By the time the litter is eight weeks of age it is entirely weaned, no longer nursing on its mother. While the puppies were nursing they received complete immunity from their mother. Once they have stopped nursing, however, they become highly susceptible to many infectious diseases. A number of these diseases can be transmitted on the hands and clothing of humans. Therefore it is extremely important that your puppy is current on all the shots it must have for its age.

A healthy Maltese puppy is a bouncy, playful extrovert. Never select a puppy that appears shy or listless because you feel sorry for it. Doing so will undoubtedly lead to heartache and expensive veterinary costs. Do not attempt to make up for what the breeder did not do in providing proper care and nutrition. It seldom works.

If at all possible take the Maltese puppy you are attracted to into a different room in the kennel or house. The smells will remain the same for the puppy so it should still feel secure but it will give you an opportunity to see how the puppy acts away from its littermates and it will also give you time to inspect the puppy more closely.

Three-day-old Maltese babies. Tiny puppies are a huge responsibility!

Even though Maltese puppies are very small they should feel sturdy to the touch. They should not feel bony nor should their abdomens be bloated and extended. A puppy that has just eaten may have a full belly, but the puppy should never appear obese.

A healthy puppy's ears will be pink and clean. Dark discharge or a bad odor could indicate ear mites, a sure sign of lack of cleanliness and poor maintenance. A Maltese puppy's breath should always smell-sweet. Its teeth must be clean and bright and there should never be any malformation of the jaw, lips or nostrils.

Maltese eyes are dark and clear—little spots of charcoal on a snow white background. Runny eyes or eyes that appear red and irritated could be caused by a myriad of problems, none of which indicate a healthy puppy.

Coughing or diarrhea are danger signals as is any discharge

from the nose or eruptions on the skin. The skin should be clean, the coat soft, clean and lustrous.

Sound conformation can be determined even at eight or ten weeks of age. The puppy's legs should be straight without bumps or malformations. The toes should point straight ahead.

The puppy's attitude tells you a great deal about its state of health. Puppies that are feeling "out of sorts" react very quickly and will usually find a warm littermate to snuggle up to and prefer to stay that way even when the rest of the "gang" wants to play or go exploring. The Maltese is an extrovert. Do not settle for anything less when selecting your puppy.

SELECTING A SHOW PROSPECT PUPPY

If you or your family are considering a show career for your puppy, we strongly advise putting yourself in the hands of an established breeder who has earned a reputation for breeding winning show dogs. He and he alone is most capable of anticipating what one might expect a young puppy of his line to develop into when it reaches maturity.

Although the potential buyer should read the American Kennel Club standard of perfection for the Maltese, it is hard for the novice to really understand the nuances of what is being asked for. The experienced breeder is best equipped to do so and will be only too happy to assist you in your quest. Even at that, no one can make accurate predictions or guarantees on a very young puppy.

Any predictions a breeder is apt to make are based upon the breeder's experience with past litters that produced winning show dogs. It should be obvious the more successful a breeder has been in producing winning Maltese through the years, the broader his or her basis of comparison will be.

The most any responsible breeder will say about a 12-week-old puppy is that it has "show potential." If you are serious about showing your Maltese, we, like most other breeders, strongly suggest

Show-quality puppies often come from top-winning show dogs. Eight-week-old Scylla's Small Kraft Regatta, "Reggie," is the son of Ch. Sand Island Small Kraft Lite.

Another offspring of the top-winning Henry, this is Scylla's Small Kraft Fortune, affectionately known as "Vanna." waiting until a puppy is from six to twelve months old before making any decisions. It only makes sense to assume that the older the puppy, the easier it will be to determine how it will turn out.

Permanent teeth come in at six months old and until that time "bites" (how the teeth are aligned) are uncertain. What looks like proper size for a show Maltese at three months can change drastically by the time the puppy matures. Coat texture can change significantly as well.

There are many other "beauty point" shortcomings a Maltese puppy might have that would in no way interfere with it being a wonderful companion, but these faults would be serious drawbacks in the show ring. Many of these flaws are such that a beginner in the breed would hardly notice. Things such as lack of pigment, one or no testicles for a male, color in the coat or an incorrect topline or tail set would not keep your

Maltese from being a happy, healthy and loving companion but these faults would keep it from ever being a winner. This is why employing the assistance of a good breeder is so important. Still, the prospective buyer should be at least generally aware of what the Maltese show puppy should look like.

All that you know regarding soundness and health of the pet puppy apply to the show puppy as well. The show prospect must not only be sound and healthy, it must adhere to the standard of the breed very closely. There are also a number of other books that can assist the newcomer in learning more about the Maltese. The more you know about the history and origin of the breed, the better equipped you will be to see the differences that distinguish the show dog from the pet.

A show puppy should at first glance have a straight silky white coat (lemon or tan on the ears is permissible), a black nose and round dark eyes with black rims. The muzzle is of medium length. The ears are low set and well feathered. The teeth must have either a scissors or level bite.

The Maltese's back is strong and straight. The tail should be carried over the back and it should lay to the

Whether you are choosing a show prospect puppy or a family pet, the Maltese you choose should look healthy and alert, and have a friendly, outgoing temperament.

If you don't have the time to housebreak and train a young puppy but still want to bring a Maltese into your life, consider adopting an adult.

side over the hindquarter. The tail should never stick up in the air.

Like the pet, the show prospect puppy must have a happy, outgoing temperament. It will be a compact little bundle of energy which, in most cases, never seems to appear out of balance. Still, there are some bloodlines that do experience an awkward stage, and if this seems to be the condition of a puppy you are considering, do mention it to the breeder. The show puppy will move around with ease and an "I love the world" attitude. Temperament of this kind is a hallmark of the breed.

PUPPY OR ADULT?

For the person anticipating a show career for his Maltese or for someone hoping to become a breeder, the purchase of a young adult provides greater certainty with respect to quality. Even those who simply want a companion could consider the adult dog.

From a breeder's point of view, Maltese act like puppies their entire lives and readily adapt to new places and people quite easily. In some instances breeders will have males or females they no longer wish to use for breeding and, after the dogs have been altered, would prefer to have them live out their lives in a private homes with all the attendant care and attention. In the private home environment the dog will become the "one and only" instead of "one of many."

Acquiring an adult dog eliminates the many problems raising a puppy involves and Maltese, unlike some other breeds, do "transfer" well. They love to be with humans and though many of us hate to admit it, most Maltese will be just as content living with one person as they are with another just so long as they are loved and well cared for.

Elderly people often prefer the adult dog, particularly one that is housebroken in that it is easier to manage and requires less supervision and damage control. Adult Maltese are seldom "chewers" and are usually more than ready to adapt to household rules.

There are things to consider, though. Adult dogs have usually developed behaviors that may or may not fit into your routine. If a Maltese has never been exposed to small children, the dog may be totally perplexed, often frightened, by this new experience. Children are also inclined to be more active and vocal than the average adult and this could intimidate the dog as well.

We strongly advise taking an adult dog on a trial basis to see if the dog will adapt to the new owner's lifestyle and environment. Most often it works, but on rare occasions a prospective owner decides training his or her dog from puppyhood is worth the time and effort it requires.

IDENTIFICATION PAPERS

The purchase of any purebred dog entitles you to three very important documents: a health record, which includes an inoculation or "shot" record; a copy of the dog's pedigree; and the registration certificate.

Inoculation Record

You will find that most Maltese breeders have initiated the necessary preliminary inoculation series for their puppies by the time they are 16 weeks of age. These inoculations temporarily protect the puppies against hepatitis, leptospirosis, distemper and canine parvovirus. "Permanent" inoculations will follow at a prescribed time. Since different breeders and veterinarians follow different approaches to inoculations, it is extremely important that the health record you obtain for your puppy accurately lists what shots have been given and when. In this way, the veterinarian you choose will be able to continue on with the appropriate inoculation series as needed. In most cases rabies inoculations are not given until a puppy is six months of age or older.

Pedigree

The pedigree is your dog's "family tree." The breeder must supply you with a copy of this document authenticating your puppy's ancestors back to at least the third generation. All purebred dogs have pedigrees. The pedigree in itself does not mean that your puppy is of show quality. All it means is that all of its ancestors were in fact registered Maltese. They may all have been of pet quality. Unscrupulous puppy dealers often try to imply that a pedigree indicates that all dogs having one are of championship caliber. This is not true. Again, it simply tells you all of the dog's ancestors are purebred.

The breeder from whom you purchase your Maltese will have started the pup's inoculations. His health record enables your veterinarian to continue his vaccination schedule.

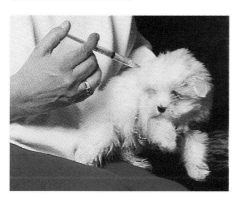

Registration Certificate

The registration certificate is the canine world's "birth certificate." This certificate is issued by a country's governing kennel club. When you transfer the ownership of your Maltese from the breeder's name to your own name, the transaction is entered on this certificate and, once mailed to the appropriate kennel club, it is permanently recorded in their computerized files.

Keep all of your dog's documents in a safe place as you will need them when you visit your veterinarian or should you ever wish to breed or show your Maltese. Keep the name, address and phone number of the breeder from whom you purchase your Maltese in a separate place as well. Should you ever lose any of these important documents, you will then be able to contact the breeder regarding obtaining duplicates.

DIET SHEET

Puppies love treats, but it takes only a few snacks to upset the balance in a small puppy's diet (and to upset his stomach!).

Your Maltese is the happy healthy puppy it is because the breeder has been carefully feeding and caring for it. Every breeder we know has his own particular way of doing this. Most breeders give the new owner a written record that details the amount and kind of food a puppy has been receiving. Do follow these recommendations to the letter at least for the first month or two after the puppy comes to live with you.

The diet sheet should indicate the number of times a day your Maltese has been accustomed to being fed and the kind of vitamin supplementation, if any, it has been receiving. Following the prescribed procedure will reduce the chance of upset stomach and loose stools.

Usually a breeder's diet sheet projects the increases and changes in food that will be necessary as your puppy grows from week to week. If the sheet does not include this information, ask the breeder for suggestions regarding increases and the eventual changeover to adult food.

In the unlikely event you are not supplied with a diet sheet by the breeder and are unable to get

The breeder's diet sheet tells the new owner what to feed to keep his pup on a balanced diet and how to adjust the type and amount of food as the pup grows.

one, your veterinarian will be able to advise you in this respect. There are countless foods now being manufactured expressly to meet the nutritional needs of puppies and growing dogs. A trip down the pet aisle at your supermarket will prove just how many choices you have. Two important tips to remember: read labels carefully for content and when dealing with established, reliable manufacturers you are more likely to get what you pay for.

HEALTH GUARANTEE

Any reputable breeder is more than willing to supply a written agreement that the purchase of your Maltese is contingent upon its passing a veterinarian's examination. Ideally you will be able to arrange an appointment with your chosen veterinarian right after you have picked up your puppy from the breeder and before you take the puppy home. If this is not possible you should not delay this procedure any longer than 24 hours from the time you take your puppy home.

TEMPERAMENT AND SOCIALIZATION

Temperament is both hereditary and environmental. Inherited good temperament can be ruined by poor treatment and lack of proper socialization. A Maltese puppy that comes from shy, nervous or aggressive stock or one that exhibits those characteristics itself will make a poor companion or show dog and should certainly never be bred from. Therefore it is critical that you obtain a happy puppy from a breeder who is determined to produce good temperaments and has taken all the necessary steps early on to provide the early socialization.

The Maltese is a breed that is known for good temperament— an easygoing, happy nature should be evident in the dog's expression.

Temperaments in the same litter can range from confident and outgoing on the high end of the scale to shy and fearful at the low end, but by and large Maltese temperament is and should be delightful. As we have stated previously, this temperament is a hallmark of the breed.

Maltese puppies will grow up to be more well adjusted if they are introduced to different people and exposed to different situations.

The Maltese is a breed that is not a particularly good one for very young children. Through no fault of their own, toddlers are not usually able to understand something as small as a Maltese must be handled with care. Care must always be taken that a puppy is not dropped or squeezed hard and that it is not left to run around where it can jump off of high things or a door might close on it.

If you are fortunate enough to have older children in the household who are of an age capable of understanding a Maltese puppy's needs, your socialization task will be assisted considerably. Maltese raised with responsible children are the best. The two seem to understand each other and in some way known only to the puppies and children themselves, they give each other the confidence to face the trying ordeal of growing up.

Every visitor who enters your household should be introduced to your Maltese. Usually this is completely unnecessary as your puppy will take care of all those formalities on its own.

Your puppy should go everywhere with you: the post office, the market, to the shopping mall—wherever. Be prepared to create a stir wherever you go because the very reason that attracted you to the first Maltese you met applies to other people as well. Everyone will want to pet your little companion and there is nothing in the world better for it.

Should your puppy back off from a stranger, pick it up and hand it to the person. The young Maltese will quickly learn all humans—young and old, short and tall and of all races, are friends.

If your Maltese has a show career in its future, there are other things in addition to just being handled that will have to be taught. All show dogs must learn to have their mouths inspected by the judge. The judge must also be able to check the teeth. Males must be accustomed to having their testicles touched as the dog show judge must determine that all male dogs are "complete," which means there are two normal-sized testicles in the scrotum. These inspections must begin in puppyhood and be done on a regular and continuing basis.

Maltese seem to be entirely compatible with other dogs as well as with humans. Their interaction with other, larger dogs must be carefully supervised, however, as other dogs are not aware of their own strength and can get entirely carried away in their enthusiasm to play. A Maltese can incite its larger canine friend into romping and playing in a manner that might well result in an unintentional accident.

THE ADOLESCENT MALTESE

At any time from about six to nine months of age the Maltese's coat may begin to change. When this happens, mats may occur where new hair growth meets already existing hair. While it does not always happen, some dogs are more prone to it than others. Thorough brushing will only take a few minutes, so it should be done every day to check on the coat's condition and keep it mat-free at this time.

It is important that you attend to these grooming sessions regularly during the early months of your puppy's growth. If your Maltese has been groomed regularly as a puppy, you will find your task is much easier when you are working with the more abundant adult coat.

Grooming your Maltese's adult coat will be much easier if you have been consistent with a grooming routine since puppyhood.

While a puppy is teething, physical changes may occur. Ears on your puppy may look high or "fly," as breeders refer to this condition. Tails can do odd things and the well placed and carried tail may suddenly be carried higher.

The adolescent Maltese seems to grow in spurts. What once looked like a nice compact puppy may look short-legged and longer-bodied at six to nine months. Usually at maturity they will regain their balanced proportions.

Ch. Sand Island Northern Lites, at ten months of age, shows every indication that she is developing a correct adult coat.

This adolescent period is a particularly important one as it is the time your Maltese must learn all the household and social rules by which it will live for the rest of its life. Your patience and commitment during this time will not only produce a respected canine good citizen but will forge a bond between the two of you that will grow and ripen into a wonderful relationship.

A show coat isn't going to keep this little guy from having a good time! He is kept in "wrappers" so he can run and play without damaging his coat.

CARING for Your Maltese

The best way to make sure your Maltese puppy is obtaining the right amount and the correct type of food for its age is to follow the diet sheet provided by the breeder from whom you obtain your puppy. Do your best not to change the puppy's diet and you will be less apt to run into digestive problems and diarrhea. Diarrhea is very serious in young puppies. Puppies with diarrhea can dehydrate very rapidly, causing severe problems and even death.

If it is necessary to change your Maltese puppy's diet for any reason, it should be done gradually over a period of several meals and a few days. Begin by adding a tablespoon or two of the new food, gradually increasing the amount until the meal consists entirely of the new product.

FEEDING THE MALTESE

At eight weeks of age, a Maltese puppy is eating four meals a day. By the time it is six months old, the puppy can do well on two meals a day with perhaps a snack in the middle of the day. If your puppy does not eat the food offered, it is either not hungry or not well. Your dog will eat when it is hungry. If you suspect the dog is not well, a trip to the veterinarian is immediately in order.

Two important things to remember when feeding your Maltese are to stick to a consistent feeding schedule and to make sure that what you feed is nutritionally complete.

By the time your Maltese is ten to twelve months old, you can reduce feedings to one or, at the most, two a day. The main meal can be given either in the morning or evening. It is really a matter of choice on your part. There are two important things to remember: feed the main meal at the same time every day and make sure what you feed is nutritionally complete.

Nutritious treats can be used to supplement your Maltese's regular meals. Remember not to overdo it; a few treats can be a lot for a small dog.

The single meal can be supplemented by a morning or nighttime snack of hard dog biscuits made especially for small dogs. These biscuits not only become highly anticipated treats by your Maltese but are genuinely helpful in maintaining healthy gums and teeth.

"Balanced" Diets

In order for a canine diet to qualify as "complete and balanced" in the United States, it must meet standards set by the Subcommittee on Canine Nutrition of the National Research Council of the National Academy of Sciences. Most commercial foods manufactured for dogs meet these standards and prove this by listing the ingredients contained in the food on every package or can. The ingredients are listed in descending order with the main ingredient listed first.

Fed with any regularity at all, refined sugars can cause your Maltese to become obese and will definitely create tooth decay. Candy stores do not exist in nature and canine teeth are not genetically disposed to handling sugars. Do not feed your Maltese candy or sweets and avoid products that contain sugar to any high degree.

Fresh water and a properly prepared balanced diet containing the essential nutrients in correct proportions are all a healthy Maltese needs to be offered. Dog foods come canned, dry, semi-moist, "scientifically fortified" and "all-natural." A visit to your local supermarket or pet store will reveal how vast an array you will be able to select from. It is important to remember that all dogs, whether toy or giant, are carnivorous (meat-eating) animals. While the vegetable content of the Maltese's diet should not be overlooked, a dog's physiology and anatomy are based upon carnivorous food acquisition. Protein and fat are absolutely essential to the well-being of your Maltese. In fact, it is wise to add a few drops of vegetable oil or bacon drippings to your dog's diet, particularly during the winter months in colder climates.

Read the list of ingredients on the dog food you buy. Animal protein should appear first on the label's list of ingredients. A base of quality kibble to which meat and even table scraps has been added can provide a nutritious meal for your Maltese.

This having been said, it should be realized that in the wild, carnivores eat the entire beast they capture and kill. The carnivore's kills consist almost entirely of herbivores (plant-eating) animals and invariably the carnivore begins its meal with the contents of the herbivore's stomach. This provides the carbohydrates, minerals and nutrients present in vegetables.

Through centuries of domestication we have made our dogs entirely dependent upon us for their well-being. Therefore we are entirely responsible for duplicating the food balance the wild dog finds in nature. The domesticated dog's diet must include protein, carbohydrates, fats, roughage and small amounts of essential minerals and vitamins.

Finding commercially prepared diets that contain all the necessary nutrients will not present a problem. It is important to understand, though, that these commercially prepared foods do contain most of the nutrients your Maltese requires. Most Maltese breeders recommend vitamin supplementation for healthy coat and increased stamina, especially for showdogs, pregnant bitches or very young puppies.

Over-Supplementation

A great deal of controversy exists today regarding the orthopedic problems that afflict many breeds. Some claim these problems are entirely hereditary conditions but many others feel they can be exacerbated by over-use of mineral and vitamin supplements for puppies. Over-supplementation is now looked upon by some breeders as a major contributor to many skeletal abnormalities found in the purebred dogs of the day. In giving vitamin supplementation one should *never* exceed the prescribed amount. No vitamin, however, is a substitute for a nutritious balanced diet.

Pregnant and lactating bitches do require supplementation of some kind but here again it is not a case of "if a little is good, a lot would be a great deal better." Extreme caution is advised in this case and best discussed with your veterinarian.

If the owner of a Maltese normally eats healthy nutritious food, there is no reason why the dog cannot be given some table scraps. What could possibly be harmful in good nutritious food? Table scraps should be given only as part of the dog's meal, and *never* from the table. A Maltese that becomes accustomed to being hand fed from the table can become a real pest at meal time very quickly. Also, guests may find the pleading stare of your little Maltese less than appealing when dinner is being served. Dogs do not care if food looks like a hot dog or a piece of cheese. Truly nutritious dog foods are seldom manufactured to look like food that appeals to humans. Dogs only care about how food smells and tastes. It is highly doubtful you will be eating your dog's food, so do not waste your money on these "looks just like" products.

Once your Maltese gets used to a feeding schedule, he'll know when it's meal time—and he'll let you know, too!

Along these lines, most of the moist foods or canned foods that have the look of "delicious red beef" look that way because they contain great amounts of red dyes. They should not be fed to a Maltese! The same coloring that makes these products look red will stain and discolor the Maltese's facial hair. Some breeders claim these products can also cause tearing, which could stain the entire face of your Maltese.

To test the dye content of either canned or dry foods, place a small amount of the moistened food after it has been prepared for your dog on an absorbent towel and allow it to remain there for several hours. If the paper is stained you can rest assured your dog's hair will be stained as well. Further, preservatives and dyes are no better for your dog than they are for you.

Special Diets

There are now any number of commercially prepared diets for dogs with special dietary needs. The overweight, underweight or geriatric dog can have its nutritional needs met as can puppies and growing dogs. The calorie content of these foods is adjusted accordingly. With the correct amount of the right foods and the proper amount of exercise, your Maltese should stay in top shape. Again, common sense must prevail. Too many calories will increase weight, too few will reduce weight.

Occasionally a young Maltese going through the teething period will become a poor eater. The concerned owner's first response is to tempt the dog by hand-feeding special treats and foods that the problem eater seems to prefer. This practice only serves to compound the problem. Once the dog learns to play the waiting game, it will turn up its nose at anything other than its favorite food knowing full well what it *wants* to eat will eventually arrive.

The Carrot Bone™ can be served as-is, in bone hard form, or can be microwaved to a biscuit consistency. It's a natural obesity and boredom fighter for your Maltese. Available at your local pet shop.

What a knockout! Here's how Scrapper likes to get his exercise—he's a top contender in the show ring and the boxing ring.

Unlike humans, dogs have no suicidal tendencies. A healthy dog will not starve itself to death. It may not eat enough to keep it in the shape we find ideal and attractive but it will definitely eat enough to maintain itself. If your Maltese is not eating properly and appears to be too thin, it is probably best to consult your veterinarian.

SPECIAL NEEDS OF THE MALTESE

Exercise

If your own exercise proclivities lie closer to a walk around the block than to 10-mile runs, your choice of a Maltese was probably a wise one. The Maltese is not a breed that requires taking your energy level to its outer limits. In fact, Maltese self-exercise if they are allowed the freedom to do so. If your Maltese shares its life with children or other dogs, it will undoubtedly be getting all the exercise it needs to stay fit, as a

Maltese is always ready for a romp or even to invent some new game that entails plenty of aerobic activity.

This does not mean that your Maltese will not benefit from a daily walk around the park or around the block. On the contrary, slow steady exercise that keeps your companion's heart rate working will do nothing but extend its life. If your Maltese is doing all this with you at its side, you are increasing the chances that the two of you will enjoy each other's company for many more years to come.

Naturally, common sense must be used concerning the extent and the intensity of the exercise you give your Maltese. A moderately fast walk for you can be considered full speed for your Maltese. Remember, young puppies have short bursts of energy and then require long rest periods. No puppy of any breed should be forced to accompany you on extended walks. Serious injuries can result. Again—short exercise periods and long rest stops for any Maltese under 10 or 12 months of age. Most adult Maltese, however, will willingly walk as far as the average owner is inclined to go.

Hot Weather

Caution must be exercised in hot weather. First of all, the Maltese is not a breed that particularly enjoys being exposed to hot summer sun. Plan your walks for the first thing in the morning if at all possible. If you cannot arrange to do this, wait until the sun has set and the outdoor temperature has dropped to a comfortable degree.

You must never leave your Maltese in a car in hot weather. Temperatures can soar in a matter of minutes and and your dog can die of heat exhaustion in less time than you would imagine. Rolling down the windows helps little and is dangerous because an over-heated Maltese will panic and might attempt to escape through the open window. A word to the wise—leave your dog at home in a cool room on hot days.

The Maltese also should not be expected to endure extremely cold weather. It is a single-coated breed and this kind of coat offers little insulation against freezing temperatures. If you are going to be outdoors for extended periods of time during extremely cold weather, you may want to consider a small coat or jacket for your dog. These are available at most pet shops and dog shows.

Do not allow your Maltese to remain wet if the two of you get caught in the rain. At the very least you should thoroughly towel-dry the wet Maltese. Better still, use your blow dryer (set on medium) to make sure your dog is thoroughly dry and mat-free.

Socialization

The Maltese is by nature a happy dog and takes most situations in stride, but it is important to accommodate the breed's natural instincts by making sure your dog is accustomed to everyday events of all kinds. Traffic, strange noises, loud or hyperactive children and strange animals can be very intimidating to a dog of any breed that has never experienced them before. Gently and gradually introduce your puppy to as many strange situations as you possibly can.

Socializing a Maltese is fun; they are real "people" dogs. Larry Abbott gets "checked out" by a curious three-week-old pup.

Make it a practice to take your Maltese with you everywhere whenever practical. The breed is a real crowd pleaser, and you will find your Maltese will savor all the attention it gets.

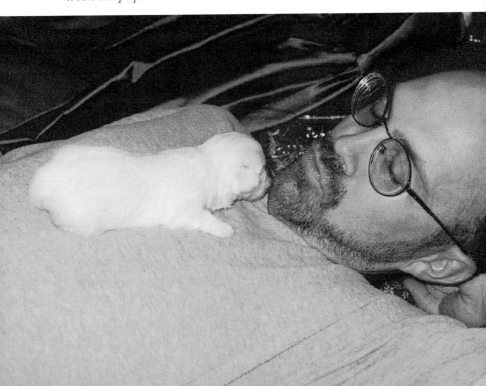

GROOMING Your Maltese

Much of what initially attracts people to the Maltese is in its sparkling white, silky coat. We wish we could tell you it does not take much to maintain that look. Unfortunately, we can't. Your Maltese will only have that special look as long as you are diligent in keeping its coat thoroughly washed and brushed. You must either learn to do this yourself or find a reliable groomer.

This cannot be accomplished by occasional attacks on the problem after long periods of neglect. Because of the mats that have developed, the damage done by neglecting the Maltese's coat can normally only be undone by shaving away the dog's entire coat. This is neither attractive nor is it good for your dog. If you are not willing to put in the time and effort necessary to maintain the Maltese's coat, which to a great extent constitutes a good part of its essence, why not get a smooth-coated dog instead? It is not necessary to maintain the *length* of coat the Maltese needs for the show ring, but maintaining the correct look of the breed is important.

Henry has the look that the Maltese is known for. His long, straight, silky white coat is in top condition and the black bows in his top knot accentuate his dark facial features.

PUPPY COAT

Undoubtedly the breeder from whom you purchased your Maltese began to accustom the puppy to grooming as soon as there was enough hair to brush. You must continue with

You will need a sturdy grooming surface, good-quality brushes, a steel comb, barber's scissors, and bows for the top knot in order to thoroughly groom your Maltese.

grooming sessions or begin them at once if for some reason they have not been started. You and your Maltese will spend many hours involved with this activity over a lifetime, so it is imperative you both learn to cooperate in the endeavor to make it an easy and pleasant experience.

The first piece of equipment you should obtain is a grooming table. A grooming table can be built or purchased at your local pet emporium. Even a sturdy snack table topped with a non-skid pad can be used as long as it is steady and does not wobble or shake. An unsteady table is a very frightening thing for any dog.

Make sure that whatever kind of table you use, it is of a height at which you can work comfortably. Adjustable-height grooming tables are available at most pet shops.

You will also need to invest in two brushes, a steel comb, barber's scissors, and a pair of nail clippers. Unless you keep your dog's coat extremely short, an electric hair dryer with heat control is a must. Electric clippers are very useful, as is a good quality spray-type coat conditioner. Consider the fact you will be using these grooming tools for many years to come, so buy the best of these items that you can afford.

A fine-tooth steel comb is helpful in removing mats and tangles from the Maltese's abundant coat.

The brush that you will need is called a pin brush, sometimes called a "Poodle brush." Another popular brush used on other breeds but which should never be used on a Maltese is a "slicker brush." The slicker can severely break the Maltese's hair and severely damage the coat. The pin brush, along with the fine-toothed comb, nail clippers and coat conditioner can be purchased at your local pet shop or at any dog show.

Do not attempt to groom your puppy on the floor. The puppy will only attempt to get away from you when it has decided enough is enough and you will end up spending a good part of your time chasing the puppy around the room. Sitting on the floor for long stretches of time is also not the most comfortable position in the world for the average adult.

The Maltese puppy should be taught to lie on its side to be groomed. As your Maltese grows and develops its adult coat, you will find the bit of effort you invested in teaching the puppy to lie on its side will be time well spent, as it will be kept in that position for most of the brushing process. Although your Maltese will also have to be kept in the standing position for some of its grooming, the lying position is a bit more difficult for the puppy to learn.

As your puppy grows and starts to develop his adult coat, you will be glad that you took the time to accustom him to grooming at an early age.

Begin this training by laying the puppy down on its side on the table. Speak reassuringly to the puppy, stroking its head and rump. Do this a number of times before you attempt to do any grooming. Repeat the process until your puppy understands what it is supposed to do when you place it on the grooming table.

To brush the puppy coat, start with the pin brush. You will then begin what is called "line brushing" at the top of the shoulder. Part the hair in a straight line from the front of the shoulder straight down to the bottom of the chest. Brush through the hair to the right and left of the part. Mist the part *The long flowing hair on the Maltese's head is called the "top knot." On show dogs, this hair is tied up and held in place with two small bows.* with an anti-static spray or conditioner. Start at the skin and brush out to the very end of the hair. Do a small section at a time and continue on down the part. When you reach the bottom of the part, return to the top and make another part just to the right of the first line you brushed. Part, brush and mist. You will repeat this process, moving each part toward the rear until you reach the puppy's tail.

I prefer to do the legs on the same side I have been working on at this time. Use the same process, parting the hair at the top of the leg and working down. Do this all around the leg and be especially careful to attend to the hard-to-reach areas under the upper legs where they join the body. Mats occur very rapidly in these areas.

Should you encounter a mat that does not brush out easily, use your fingers and the steel comb to help separate the hairs as much as possible. Do not cut or pull out the matted hair. Apply coat conditioner directly to the mat and brush completely from the skin out.

When you have finished the legs on the one side, turn the puppy over and complete the entire process on the other side–*part, brush and spray.* As your Maltese becomes accustomed to this process, you may find the puppy considers this nap time. You may have to lift your puppy into the standing position to arouse it from its slumber.

With the puppy standing, do the chest and tail. When brushing, do so gently so as not to break the hair. When brushing on and around the rear legs, make sure to give special

attention to the area of the anus and genitalia. Needless to say, it is important to be extremely careful when brushing in these areas because they are very sensitive and easily injured.

Use your fine-toothed comb around the face, being very careful not to catch the eye rim or poke the eye. Check for stains at this time as well. If there are stains, use dry cornstarch on dry or slightly damp hair around the eyes. This will help lighten the stain. Rub in the cornstarch and then comb most of it out. Do not use baby powder. Baby powder gums the hair—cornstarch absorbs.

NAIL TRIMMING

This is a good time to accustom your Maltese to having its nails trimmed and having its feet inspected. Always inspect your dog's feet for cracked pads. If your Maltese is allowed out in the yard or accompanies you to the park or woods, check between the toes for splinters and thorns. Pay particular attention to any swollen or tender areas. In many sections of the country there is a weed called a "fox tail," which releases a small barbed hook that carries its seed. This hook easily finds its way into a dog's foot or between its toes and works its way deep into the dog's flesh. This will very quickly cause soreness and infection. These barbs should be removed by your veterinarian before serious problems result.

The nails of a Maltese who spends most of its time indoors or on grass when outdoors can grow long very quickly. If you allow the nails to become overgrown, don't expect to be able to cut them back easily. Each nail has a blood vessel running through the center called the "quick." The quick grows close

"Wrapping" is a necessity if the Maltese's coat is to grow to full length. If not wrapped properly, the delicate hair can easily break or be damaged.

to the end of the nail and contains very sensitive nerve endings. If the nail is allowed to grow too long it will be impossible to cut it back to a proper length without cutting into the quick. This causes severe pain to the dog and can also result in a great deal of bleeding that can be very difficult to stop.

Any stains around the face can be lightened by applying cornstarch to the stained hair and gently combing it out.

Should the quick be nipped in the trimming process, there are any number of blood clotting products available at pet shops that will almost immediately stem the flow of blood. It is wise to have one of these products on hand in case there is a nail trimming accident or the dog tears a nail on its own.

Your Maltese will have to get used to having his nails trimmed and his feet checked. The earlier you start this routine, the easier it will be.

GROOMING THE ADULT MALTESE

Ideally you and your Maltese have spent the many months between puppyhood and full maturity learning to assist each other through the grooming process. The two of you have survived the changing of the puppy coat and the arrival of the entirely different adult hair. The hair of the adult Maltese is more profuse and if allowed to grow unchecked, will become very long.

The method of brushing the adult coat is the same as that used since your Maltese was a puppy. The only real difference is that you have a bit more dog and the hair itself will be longer unless you cut it back.

While one might expect grooming an adult Maltese to be a monumental task, this is not necessarily so. The important thing is consistency. A few minutes a day, every day, precludes your dog's hair becoming a tangled mess, which may take you hours to undo. You should have been practicing the brushing routine for so long it has undoubtedly become second nature to both of you.

Ch. Shanlyn's Rais'n A Raucous ("Scrapper") is in top show condition with his fully groomed coat.

Here, Scrapper models his pet clip, which obviously requires much less maintenance than the full show coat.

Some owners take great pride in keeping the coat of their Maltese long and flowing. This, of course, is an absolute requirement if you wish to show your Maltese. It is possible to grow a very long coat on your Maltese but unless the coat is "wrapped" it can prove to be a hardship on both you and your dog. Wrapping a coat must be done properly in order to accomplish your goal and we highly recommend seeking the assistance of the breeder from who you purchased your Maltese or a professional groomer.

Most pet owners, however, find this an extremely demanding task and keep the coat cut back to a moderate length. Scissors can be used to cut the coat back to a manageable length and the electric clippers can be used to remove the hair from the frequently matted "arm pits" (under the legs where they join the body) and under the the dog's stomach.

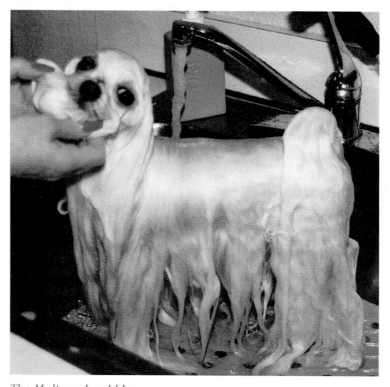

The Maltese should be rinsed very thoroughly after shampooing—any residue can dry the coat and cause a skin irritation.

If you do not care to keep the coat long, a Maltese can be kept in a very cute "puppy trim." The body is clipped with the electric clippers using a number-four blade. The ears, whiskers and tail are left longer so as to maintain the distinctive Maltese look.

Hair should be removed from between the toe pads. You can use barber scissors or electric clippers to accomplish this.

BATHING YOUR MALTESE

Bathe the Maltese once a week or whenever needed. Use a quality shampoo made especially for white dogs. A Maltese should never be bathed until after it has been thoroughly brushed. If all mats are are not out before you bathe, your dog will end up looking like a cotton ball! Mats only get worse when doused with water.

A small cotton ball placed inside each ear will avoid water running down into the dog's ear canal and a drop or two of mineral oil or a dab of Vaseline placed in each eye will prevent shampoo irritation.

A rubber mat should be placed at the bottom of the tub so that your dog does not slip and become frightened. A rubber spray hose is absolutely necessary to remove all shampoo residue. Rinse thoroughly, apply a quality coat conditioner and rinse again.

In bathing, start behind the ears and work back. Finally, carefully wash around the face, being very careful not to get suds into your dog's eyes. Rinse well. Shampoo residue in the coat is sure to dry the hair and could cause skin irritation.

As soon as you have completed the bath, use a heavy towel to remove as much of the excess water as possible. Your Maltese will undoubtedly assist you in the process by shaking a great deal of the water out of the coat on its own.

A Maltese's coat must be "brush dried," using a pin brush and a blow dryer on the medium setting, to attain the proper straight, silky look.

USING A HAIR DRYER

It is very important to gently "brush dry" your Maltese using your pin brush and a hair dryer to give it the straight, silky look that is proper. Always set your hair dryer at "medium" setting, never "hot." The hot setting may be quicker but it will also dry out the hair and could easily burn the delicate skin of your Maltese.

Keep the ears clean by putting a little ear cleanser in the ear and wiping the ear with a tissue. Do not probe into the ear beyond where you can see! The delicate ear drum can be easily injured. If you suspect a problem further on down in the ear canal, consult your veterinarian.

HOUSEBREAKING and Training Your Maltese

There is no breed of dog that cannot be trained. It does appear some breeds are more difficult to get the desired response from than others. In many cases, however, this has more to do with the trainer and his or her training methods than to the dog's inability to learn. With the proper approach, any dog can be taught to be a good canine citizen. Many dog owners do not understand how a dog learns nor do they realize they can be breed specific in their approach to training.

Young puppies have an amazing capacity to learn. This capacity is greater than most humans realize. It is important to remember, though, these young puppies also forget with great speed unless they are reminded of what they have learned by continual reinforcement.

As puppies leave the nest they begin their search for two things: a pack leader and rules set down by that leader by which they can abide. Because puppies, particularly Maltese puppies, are cuddly, cute and very small, their owners fail miserably in supplying these very basic needs. Instead, the owner immediately begins to respond to the demands of the puppy.

For example, a puppy quickly learns it will be allowed into the house or a room because it is barking or whining, not because it can only enter the house when it is not barking or whining. Instead of learning the only way it will be fed is to follow a set procedure (i.e., sitting or lying down on command), it learns leaping about the kitchen or barking incessantly is what gets results.

If the young puppy cannot find its pack leader in an owner, the puppy assumes the role of pack leader. Yes, even as small as that bit of fluff is, if there are no rules, the Maltese puppy learns to make its own. Unfortunately, the negligent owner continually reinforces the puppy's decisions by allowing it to govern the household. With small dogs like the Maltese, this scenario can produce a neurotic nuisance. In large dogs, the situation can be downright dangerous. Neither situation is an acceptable one.

The key to successful training lies in establishing the proper relationship between dog and owner. The owner or family must be the pack leader(s) and the individual or family must provide the rules by which the dog abides. Once this is established, ease of training depends in a great part upon just how much a dog depends upon its master's approval. The entirely dependent dog lives to please its master and will do everything in its power to evoke the approval response from the person it is devoted to.

At the opposite end of the pole we have the totally independent dog who is not remotely concerned with what its master thinks or wants. Dependency varies from one breed to the next and, to a degree, within breeds as well. Maltese are no exception to this rule. Fortunately for the owner of a Maltese, however, the breed really wants to please.

Three-month-old Daisy has staked her claim to a spot on the couch. If you don't want your Maltese on the furniture, set the rules before she has a chance to get comfortable.

HOUSEBREAKING

A major key to successfully training your Maltese, whether it is obedience training or housebreaking, is *avoidance.* It is much easier for your Maltese to learn something if you do not first have to have it unlearn some bad habit. The crate-training method of housebreaking is a highly successful method of avoiding bad habits before they begin.

First-time dog owners are inclined to initially see the crate method of housebreaking as cruel, but those same people will return later and thank us profusely for having suggested it in the first place. They are also surprised to find that the puppy will eventually come to think of its crate as a place of private retreat—a den to which it will retreat for rest and privacy. The success of the crate method is based upon the fact that puppies will not soil the area in which they sleep unless they are forced to.

Use of a crate reduces house training time to an absolute minimum and avoids keeping a puppy under

Crate training isn't cruel; rather, it gives your pup a place to call her own. Daisy is right at home in her soft doggie bed, cuddling with some of her friends.

Fiberglass crates, the kind that are used by airlines, are popular with many Maltese owners. A soft blanket or pad on the bottom helps to make the dog more comfortable.

constant stress by incessantly correcting it for making mistakes in the house. The anti-crate advocates consider it cruel to confine a puppy for any length of time but find no problem in constantly harassing and punishing the puppy because it has wet on the carpet and relieved itself behind the sofa.

Crates come in a wide variety of styles. The fiberglass shipping kennels used by many airlines are popular with many Maltese owners, but residents of the extremely warm climates sometimes prefer the wire crate type. Both are available at pet stores.

The crate used for housebreaking should only be large enough for the puppy to stand up and lie down in and stretch out comfortably. There are many sizes to choose from. We

Seven-week-old "Dixie" is wide awake and ready to play! Keep an eye on your pup—after waking from a nap, she will need to be taken outside to relieve herself.

advise using the small-sized airline-type crate. This size seems ideal for most Maltese.

Begin using the crate as a place to feed your Maltese puppy. Keep the door closed and latched while the puppy is eating. When the meal is finished, open the crate and carry the puppy outdoors to the spot where you want it to learn to eliminate. In the event you do not have outdoor access or will be away from home for long periods of time, begin housebreaking by placing newspapers in some out of the way corner that is easily accessible for the puppy. If you consistently take your puppy to the same spot you will reinforce the habit of going there for that purpose.

It is important that you do not let the puppy loose after eating. Young puppies will eliminate almost immediately after eating or drinking. They will also be ready to relieve themselves when they first wake up and after playing. If you keep a watchful eye on your puppy you will quickly learn when this is about to take place. A puppy usually circles and sniffs the floor just before it will relieve itself. Do not give your puppy an opportunity to learn that it can eliminate in the house! Your housetraining chores will be reduced considerably if you avoid this happening in the first place.

If you are not able to watch your puppy every minute, it should be in its crate with the door securely latched. Each time you put your puppy in the crate, give it a small treat of some kind. Throw the treat to the back of the crate and encourage the puppy to walk in on its own. When it does so, praise the puppy and perhaps hand it another piece of the treat through the opening in the front of the crate.

Seven-week-old "Frank" curls up in a cozy corner of his crate. Once your puppy is used to his crate, it will become his private "den" where he can retreat and relax.

Do not succumb to your puppy's complaints about being in its crate. The puppy must learn to stay there and to do so without unnecessary complaining. A quick "no" command and a tap on the crate will usually get the puppy to understand theatrics will not result in liberation. (Remember, as the pack leader, you make the rules and the puppy is seeking to learn what they are!)

Do understand a puppy of 8 to 12 weeks will not be able to contain itself for long periods of time. Puppies of that age must relieve themselves every few hours, except at night. Your schedule must be adjusted accordingly. Also make sure your puppy has relieved its bowel and bladder the last thing at night, and do not hesitate to take your puppy out first thing when you wake up in the morning.

Your first priority in the morning is to get the puppy outdoors. Just how early this ritual will take place will depend much more upon your puppy than upon you. If your Maltese is like most others there will be no doubt in your mind when it needs to be let out. You will also very quickly learn to tell the difference between the "this is an emergency" complaint and the "I just want out" grumbling. Do not test the young puppy's ability to contain itself. Its vocal demands to be let out is confirmation that the housebreaking lesson is being learned.

Should you find it necessary to be away from home all day, you will not be able to leave your puppy in a crate. On the other hand, do not make the mistake of allowing it to roam the house or even a large room at will. Confine the puppy to a very small room or partitioned area and cover the floor with newspaper. Make this area large enough so that the puppy will not have to relieve itself next to its bed, food bowl or water bowl. You will soon find the puppy will be inclined to use one particular spot to perform its bowel and bladder functions. When you are home you must take the puppy to this exact spot to eliminate at the appropriate time.

BASIC TRAINING

Your emotional state and the environment in which you train are just as important to training as is your dog's state of mind at the time. Never begin training when you are irritated, distressed or preoccupied. Nor should you begin basic training in a place that interferes with you or your dog's concentration. Once the commands are understood and learned you can begin testing your dog in public places, but at first the two of you should work in a place where you can concentrate fully upon each other.

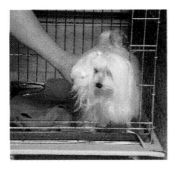

You must stay aware of the sensitivity level of your Maltese and its desire to please. Maltese

Your Maltese wants to keep his crate clean, so listen to him for signs that he needs to go out. If you ignore his warning and he has an accident, you will be the one to blame.

74

Your Maltese will be sure to tell you when he needs to go out— and he'll let you know when he's ready to come back in!

respond well to lots of praise but do not respond to yelling or being struck. Never resort to shaking or striking your Maltese puppy. A very stern "no" is usually more than sufficient and even in the most persistent unwanted behavior, striking the ground with a rolled-up newspaper is about as extreme as you will ever need to be.

The extent to which the breed can be trained knows few limits. The American Maltese Association issues awards to Maltese that gain all the obedience titles offered by the American Kennel Club: Companion Dog, Companion Dog Excellent and the advanced degrees for Utility Dog and Utility Dog Excellent. Do not feel limited by the diminutive size of the Maltese. The breed's ability to learn and perform far exceeds its size.

The "No" Command

There is no doubt whatsoever one of the most important commands your Maltese puppy will ever learn is the meaning of the "no" command. It is critical that the puppy learn this as soon as possible. One important piece of advice in using this and all other commands—*never give a command you are not prepared and able to enforce!* A good leader does not enforce rules arbitrarily. The only way a puppy learns to obey commands is to realize that once issued, commands must be complied with. Learning the "no" command should start on the first day of the puppy's arrival at your home.

Be fair to your dog. It can easily learn the difference between things it can and cannot do. A dog is not able to learn that there are some things it can do one time but not the next. Yelling at your dog for lying on the bed today when it was perfectly all right for it to do so the previous day serves only to confuse.

Leash Training

Begin leash training by putting a soft lightweight collar on your puppy. After a few hours of occasional scratching at the unaccustomed addition, your puppy will quickly forget it is even there.

Begin getting your puppy accustomed to its collar by leaving it on for a few minutes at a time. Gradually extend the time you leave the collar on. Once this is accomplished, attach a lightweight leash to the collar while you are playing with the puppy. Do not try to guide the puppy at first. You are only trying to get the puppy used to having something attached to the collar.

It may not be necessary for the puppy or adult Maltese to wear its collar and identification tags within the confines of your home later, but no Maltese should ever leave home without a collar and

The first step in leash training: put a light collar or harness on your pup, without the leash attached, and let him wear it around the house for short periods of time.

without the attached leash held securely in your hand.

Get your puppy to follow you as you move around by coaxing it along with a treat of some kind. Let the puppy smell what you have in your hand and then move a few steps back, holding the treat in front of the puppy's nose. Just as soon as the puppy takes a few steps toward you, praise it enthusiastically and continue to do so as you to move along.

Make the first few lessons brief and fun for the puppy. Continue the lessons in your home or yard until the puppy is completely unconcerned about the fact that it is on a leash. With a treat in one hand and the leash in the other you can begin to use both to guide the puppy in the direction you wish to go. Eventually the two of you can venture out on the sidewalk in front of your house and then on to adventures everywhere! This is one lesson no puppy is too young to learn.

Encourage your pup to come to you as often as possible and always greet him with a friendly voice and lots of petting. This will build a foundation for teaching the recall.

The "Come" Command

The next most important lesson for the Maltese puppy to learn is to come when called; therefore, it is very important that the puppy learn its name as soon as possible. Constant repetition is what does the trick in teaching a puppy its name. Use the name every time you talk to your puppy. There is a quotation we particularly like that appeared in an old British dog book we found regarding conversations with our canine friends. It states simply, "Of course you should talk to your dogs. But talk sense!"

Learning to "come" on command could save your dog's life when the two of you venture out into the world. "Come" is the command a dog must understand has to be obeyed without question but the dog should not associate that command with fear. Your dog's response to its name and the word "come" should always be associated with a pleasant experience such as great praise, petting or even a food treat.

Again, remember it is much easier to avoid the establishment of bad habits than it is to correct them once set. Never give the "come" command unless you are sure your puppy will come to you.

The very young puppy is far more inclined to respond to the "come" command than the older dog. Young puppies are entirely dependent upon you. An older dog may lose some of that dependency and become preoccupied with its surroundings. So start your "come" command training early on.

You may want to begin teaching the recall with your Maltese pup on a leash—this will help ensure the correct response in the early stages of training.

Use the command initially when the puppy is already on its way to you or give the command while walking or running away from the youngster. Clap your hands and sound very happy and excited about having the puppy join in on this "game."

The very young Maltese puppy will normally want to stay as close to its owner as possible, especially in strange surroundings. When your puppy sees you moving away, its natural inclination will be to get close to you. This is a perfect time to use the "come" command.

You may want to attach a long leash or light rope to the puppy's collar to ensure the correct response. Do not chase or punish your puppy for not obeying the "come" command. Doing so in the initial stages of training makes the youngster associate the command with something to fear and this will result in avoidance rather than the immediate positive response you desire. It is imperative that you praise your Maltese puppy and give it a treat when it does come to you, even if it voluntarily delays responding for many minutes.

The "Sit" and "Stay" Commands

Just as important to your Maltese puppy's safety as the "no" command and learning to come when called are the "sit" and "stay" commands. Even very young Maltese can learn the sit command quickly, especially if it appears to be a game and a food treat is involved.

First, remember the Maltese-in-training should always be on collar and leash for all its lessons. A Maltese puppy is curious

about everything that goes on around it and a puppy is not beyond getting up and walking away when it has decided it needs to investigate something.

Give the "sit" command just before you reach down and exert pressure on your puppy's rear. Praise the puppy profusely when it does sit, even though it was you who exerted the effort. A food treat of some kind always seems to make the experience that more enjoyable for the puppy.

Continue holding the dog's rear end down and repeat the "sit" command several times. If your puppy makes an attempt to get up, repeat the command yet again while exerting pressure on the rear end until the correct position is assumed. Make your puppy stay in this position a little bit longer with each succeeding lesson. Begin with a few seconds and increase the time as lessons progress over the following weeks.

The "down" command may be harder to teach than the "sit," as "down" is a somewhat submissive position.

Should your puppy attempt to get up or to lie down it should be corrected by simply saying "sit!" in a firm voice. This should be accompanied by returning the dog to the desired position. Only when you decide your dog should get up should it be allowed to do so. Do not test the extent of your young Maltese puppy's patience. Remember you are dealing with a baby and the attention span of any youngster is relatively limited. When you do decide the dog can get up, call its name, say "OK" and make a big fuss over it. Praise and a food treat are in order every time your Maltese responds correctly.

Once your puppy has mastered the "sit" lesson you may start on the "stay" command. With your Maltese on leash and facing you, command it to "sit," then take a step or two back. If your dog attempts to get up to follow, firmly say, "sit, stay!" with your hand raised, palm toward the dog.

Praise is in order every time your Maltese obeys a command. A food treat can also be used as a reward for a job well done.

If your dog attempts to get up you must correct it at once, returning it to the sit position and repeating "stay!" Once your Maltese begins to understand what you want, you can gradually increase the distance you step back. With a long leash attached to your dog's collar, start with a few steps and gradually increase the distance to several yards. It is important for your Maltese to learn that the "sit, stay" command must be obeyed no matter how far away you are. With advanced training your Maltese can be taught the command is to be obeyed even when you leave the room or are entirely out of sight.

As your Maltese becomes accustomed to responding to this lesson and is able to remain in the sit position for as long as you command, do not end the command by calling the dog to you. Walk back to your Maltese and say "OK." This will let your dog know the command is over. Once your Maltese becomes entirely dependable, you can then call the dog to you.

The "sit, stay" command can take considerable time and patience to get across to puppies. You must not forget their attention span will be short. Keep the "stay" part of the lesson very short until your puppy is about six months old.

The "Down" Command

Do not try and teach your Maltese puppy too many things at once. Wait until you have mastered one lesson quite well before moving on to something new.

When you feel quite confident that your puppy is comfortable with the "sit" and "stay" commands, you can start work on "down." This is the single word command for "lie down." Use the "down" command *only* when you want the dog to lie down. If you want your Maltese to get off your sofa or to stop jumping up on people, use the "off" command. Do not interchange these two commands. Doing so will only serve to confuse your dog and evoking the right response will become next to impossible.

The "down" position is especially useful if you want your Maltese to remain in one place for a long period of time. Most dogs are far more inclined to stay put when lying down than when they are sitting or standing.

Teaching this command to your Maltese may take more time and patience than the previous lessons the two of you have undertaken. It is believed by some animal behaviorists that assuming the "down" position somehow represents greater submissiveness.

With your Maltese sitting in front of and facing you, hold a treat in your right hand with the excess part of the leash in your left hand. Hold the treat under the dog's nose and slowly bring your hand down to the ground. Your dog will follow the treat with its head and neck. As it does, give the command "down" and exert *light* pressure on the dog's shoulders with your left hand. If your dog resists the pressure on its shoulders *do not continue pushing down;* doing so will only create more resistance. Reach down and slide the dog's feet toward you until it is lying down.

An alternative method of getting your Maltese headed into the down position is to move around to the dog's right side and as you draw its attention downward with your right hand, slide your left hand under the dog's front legs and gently slide them forward. You will undoubtedly have to be on your knees next to the youngster in order to do this.

As your dog's forelegs begin to slide out to its front, keep moving the treat along the ground until the dog's whole body is lying on the ground while you continually repeat "down." Once your dog has assumed the position you desire, give it the treat and a lot of praise. Continue assisting your Maltese into the "down" position until it does so on its own. Be firm and be patient.

The "Heel" Command

In learning to heel, your Maltese will walk on your left side with its shoulder next to your leg no matter which direction you might go or how quickly you turn. Learning this command can be an extremely valuable lesson for your dog. A Maltese that darts back and forth in front of or under its master's feet can endanger itself and cause serious injury for its owner as well.

Your Maltese will be more likely to stay put if he is lying down rather than sitting or standing.

Teaching your Maltese to heel is critical to off-leash control and will not only make your daily walks far more enjoyable, it will make a far more tractable companion when the two of you are in crowded or confusing situations. We do not recommend ever allowing your Maltese to be off leash when you are away from home but it is important to know you can control your dog no matter what the circumstances are.

A lightweight, rounded leather collar or a small jeweler's snake chain are best for training long-haired toy dogs, especially for the heeling lesson. Changing from the collar your dog regularly wears to something different indicates what you are doing is "business" and not just a casual stroll. The pet shop at which you purchase your other supplies can assist you

in selecting the best training collar that will help you with your lessons but not catch in your dog's hair.

As you train your Maltese puppy to walk along on the leash, you should accustom the youngster to walk on your left side. The leash should cross your body from the dog's collar to your right hand. The excess portion of the leash will be folded into your right hand and your left hand on the leash will be used to make corrections with the leash.

A quick, gentle jerk on the leash with your left hand will keep your dog from lunging side to side, pulling ahead or darting between your legs. As you make a correction, give the "heel" command. Keep the leash loose when your dog maintains the proper position at your side.

If your dog begins to drift away, give the leash a quick jerk and guide the dog back to the correct position and give the "heel" command. Do not pull on the lead with steady pressure. What is needed is a sharp but gentle jerking motion to get your dog's attention.

The Maltese is a highly trainable breed, due to his easygoing nature and his instinctive desire to please his master.

TRAINING CLASSES

There are few limits to what a patient, consistent Maltese owner can teach his or her dog. Maltese are highly trainable. Remember the breed's life-long history of striving to please. Once lessons are mastered you will find most Maltese will perform with enthusiasm and gusto that make all the hard work well worth while.

For advanced obedience work beyond the basics it is wise for the Maltese owner to consider local professional assistance. Professional trainers have had long-standing experience in avoiding the pitfalls of obedience training and can help you to avoid them as well.

The clever Maltese can be taught many things beyond the basic commands. Serenade stands up on her hind legs to get a tasty treat.

This training assistance can be obtained in many ways. Classes are particularly good in that your dog is learning to obey commands in spite of all the interesting sights and smells of other dogs. There are free classes at many parks and recreation facilities, as well as very formal and sometimes very expensive individual lessons with private trainers. However, having someone else train the dog for you would be last on our list of recommendations. The rapport that develops between the owner who has trained his or her Maltese and the dog itself is incomparable. The effort you expend to teach your dog to be a pleasant companion and good canine citizen pays off in years of enjoyable companionship.

Scrapper was the #1 Maltese and #1 Toy Dog in 1994. Bred by Linda Podgurski. Owned by Vicki Abbott, Sharon and David Newcomb, and Joseph F. Joly, III.

VERSATILITY

There is no end to the number of activities you and your Maltese can enjoy together. The breed is highly successful in both conformation shows and obedience trials.

There are Canine Good Citizen certificates that can be earned through the American Kennel Club, and a new event called agility. Agility courses are actually "obstacle courses" for dogs and are not only fun for dog and owner but Maltese owners find their little dogs enjoy some of the exercises as much as they do.

Owners not inclined toward competitive events might find enjoyment in having their Maltese serve as therapy dogs. Dogs used in this area are trained to assist the sick, the elderly and often the handicapped.

Maltese have proven themselves to be of outstanding assistance to the hearing impaired. Signaling their owners at the sound of the phone, the door bell or someone knocking or calling can be a wonderful addition to someone's life.

One of our little dogs lives in Maryland as a hearing assistance dog. He completed training so that he could let his owner know a whole myriad of things including alerting her when the smoke alarm goes off. His owner says he is performing very well!

Other therapy dogs make visits to hospitals and homes for the aged. It has been proven these visits provide great therapeutic value to patients.

The well-trained Maltese can provide a whole world of activities for the owner. You are limited only by the amount of time you wish to invest in this remarkable breed.

SPORT of Purebred Dogs

Welcome to the exciting and sometimes frustrating sport of dogs. No doubt you are trying to learn more about dogs or you wouldn't be deep into this book. This section covers the basics that may entice you, further your knowledge and help you to understand the dog world. If you decide to give showing, obedience or any other dog activities a try, then I suggest you seek further help from the appropriate source.

Dog showing has been a very popular sport for a long time and has been taken quite seriously by some. Others only enjoy it as a hobby.

The Kennel Club in England was formed in 1859, the American Kennel Club was established in 1884 and the Canadian Kennel Club was formed in 1888. The purpose of these clubs was to register purebred dogs and maintain their Stud Books. In the beginning, the concept of registering dogs was not readily accepted. More than 36 million dogs have been enrolled in the AKC Stud Book since its inception in 1888. Presently the kennel clubs not only register dogs but adopt and enforce rules and regulations governing dog shows, obedience trials and field trials. Over the years they have fostered and encouraged interest in the health and welfare of the purebred

Ch. Melody Lane Sings O' Al-Mar Luv wins the American Maltese Association's National specialty. Bred by Marge Lewis, owned by Mariko Sukezaki, handled by the author.

dog. They routinely donate funds to veterinary research for study on genetic disorders.

Below are the addresses of the kennel clubs in the United States, Great Britain and Canada.

The American Kennel Club
51 Madison Avenue
New York, NY 10010
(Their registry is located at: 5580 Centerview Drive, STE 200, Raleigh, NC 27606-3390)

The Maltese's beauty and outgoing temperament make him a favorite in the show ring.

The Kennel Club
1 Clarges Street
Piccadilly, London, WIY 8AB, England

The Canadian Kennel Club
111 Eglinton Avenue
East Toronto, Ontario M6S 4V7
Canada

Today there are numerous activities that are enjoyable for both the dog and the handler. Some of the activities include conformation showing, obedience competition, tracking, agility, the Canine Good Citizen Certificate, and a wide range of instinct tests that vary from breed to breed. Where you start depends upon your goals which early on may not be readily apparent.

Puppy Kindergarten

Every puppy will benefit from this class. PKT is the foundation for all future dog activities from conformation to "couch potatoes." Pet owners should make an effort to attend even if they never expect to show their dog. The class is designed for puppies about three months of age with graduation at approximately five months of age. All the puppies will be in the same age group and, even though some may be a little unruly, there should not be any real problem.

This class will teach the puppy some beginning obedience. As in all obedience classes the owner learns how to train his own dog. The PKT class gives the puppy the opportunity to interact with other puppies in the same age group and exposes him to strangers, which is very important. Some dogs grow up with behavior problems, one of them being fear of strangers. As you can see, there can be much to gain from this class.

CONFORMATION

Conformation showing is our oldest dog show sport. This type of showing is based on the dog's appearance—that is his structure, movement and attitude. When considering this type of showing, you need to be aware of your breed's standard and be able to evaluate your dog compared to that standard. The breeder of your puppy or other experienced breeders would be good sources for such an evaluation. Puppies can go through lots of changes over a period of time. I always say most puppies start out as promising hopefuls and then after maturing may be disappointing as show candidates. Even so this should not deter them from being excellent pets.

Usually conformation training classes are offered by the local kennel or obedience clubs. These are excellent places for training puppies. The puppy should be able to walk on a lead before entering such a class. Proper ring procedure and technique for posing (stacking) the dog will be demonstrated as well as gaiting the dog. Usually certain patterns are used in the ring such as the triangle or the "L." Conformation class, like

Ch. Sand Island Small Kraft Lite, "Henry," is presented by the author at a Beverly Hills Kennel Club show.

the PKT class, will give your youngster the opportunity to socialize with different breeds of dogs and humans too.

It takes some time to learn the routine of conformation showing. Usually one starts at the puppy matches which may be AKC Sanctioned or Fun Matches. These matches are generally for puppies from two or three months to a year old, and there may be classes for the adult over the age of 12 months.

Henry is gaited in the ring at Westminster by his handler, author Vicki Abbott.

Ch. Scylla's Starfire's Mina Mina, handled by Jere Olson to her championship under judge Lois Wolff White. Bred by Larry and Vicki Abbott.

Similar to point shows, the classes are divided by sex and after completion of the classes in that breed or variety, the class winners compete for Best of Breed or Variety.

BEST OF OPP. SEX
SIOUX VALLEY K.C.
MAY 27, 1990
OLSON PHOTO
NEW CHAMPION

The winner goes on to compete in the Group and the Group winners compete for Best in Match. No championship points are awarded for match wins.

A few matches can be great training for puppies even though there is no intention to go on showing. Matches enable the puppy to meet new people and be handled by a stranger—the judge. It is also a change of environment, which broadens the horizon for both dog and handler. Matches and other dog activities boost the confidence of the handler and especially the younger handlers.

Puppy matches can be a great start to a show career and a confidence booster for the dog. This young Maltese gets a pre-show touch-up to look his best.

Earning an AKC championship is built on a point system, which is different from Great Britain. To become an AKC Champion of Record the dog must earn 15 points. The number of points earned each time depends upon the number of dogs in competition. The number of points available at each show depends upon the breed, its sex and the location of the show. The United States is divided into ten AKC zones. Each zone has its own set of points. The purpose of the zones is to try to equalize the points available from breed to breed and area to area.The AKC adjusts the point scale annually.

The number of points that can be won at a show are between one and five. Three-, four- and five-point wins are considered majors. Not only does the dog need 15 points won under three different judges, but those points must include two majors under two different judges. Canada also works on a point system but majors are not required.

Dogs always show before bitches. The classes available to those seeking points are: Puppy (which may be divided into 6 to 9 months and 9 to 12 months); 12 to 18 months; Novice; Bred-by-Exhibitor; American-bred; and Open. The class winners of the same sex of each breed or variety compete against each other for Winners Dog and Winners Bitch. A Reserve Winners Dog and Reserve

A windy day cannot spoil the beauty of a top-quality Maltese like Henry.

Winners Bitch are also awarded but do not carry any points unless the Winners win is disallowed by AKC. The Winners Dog and Bitch compete with the specials (those dogs that have attained championship) for Best of Breed or Variety, Best of Winners and Best of Opposite Sex. It is possible to pick up an extra point or even a major if the points are higher for the defeated winner than those of Best of Winners. The latter would get the higher total from the defeated winner.

Vicki Abbott and Ch. Sand Island Small Kraft Lite, winning the Toy Group at Westminster in 1992 under judge Dawn Vick Hansen.

At an all-breed show, each Best of Breed or Variety winner will go on to his respective Group and then the Group winners will compete against each other for Best in Show. There are seven Groups: Sporting, Hounds, Working, Terriers, Toys, Non-Sporting and Herding. Obviously there are no Groups at specialty shows (those shows that have only one breed or a show such as the American Spaniel Club's Flushing Spaniel Show, which is for all flushing spaniel breeds).

Earning a championship in England is somewhat different since they do not have a point system. Challenge Certificates are awarded if the judge feels the dog is deserving regardless of the number of dogs in competition. A dog must earn three Challenge Certificates under three different judges, with at least one of these Certificates being won after the age of 12 months. Competition is very strong and entries may be higher than they are in the U.S. The Kennel Club's Challenge Certificates are only available at Championship Shows.

In England, The Kennel Club regulations require that certain dogs, Border Collies and Gundog breeds, qualify in a working capacity (i.e., obedience or field trials) before becoming a full Champion. If they do not qualify in the working aspect, then they are designated a Show Champion, which is equivalent to the AKC's Champion of Record. A Gundog may be granted the title of Field Trial Champion (FT Ch.) if it passes all the tests in the field but would also have to qualify in conformation before becoming a full Champion. A Border Collie that earns the title of Obedience Champion (Ob Ch.) must also qualify in the conformation ring before becoming a Champion.

The U.S. doesn't have a designation full Champion but does award for Dual and Triple Champions. The Dual Champion

GROUP
FIRST

THE
WESTMINSTER
KENNEL CLUB

ARY 10 & 11, 1992

must be a Champion of Record, and either Champion Tracker, Herding Champion, Obedience Trial Champion or Field Champion. Any dog that has been awarded the titles of Champion of Record, and any two of the following: Champion Tracker, Herding Champion, Obedience Trial Champion or Field Champion, may be designated as a Triple Champion.

The shows in England seem to put more emphasis on breeder judges than those in the U.S. There is much competition within the breeds. Therefore the quality of the individual breeds should be very good. In the United States we tend to have more "all around judges" (those that judge multiple breeds) and use the breeder judges at the specialty shows. Breeder judges are more familiar with their own breed since they are actively breeding that breed or did so at one time. Americans emphasize Group and Best in Show wins and promote them accordingly.

The Westminster Kennel Club dog show is the oldest show in the United States. It is held annually at Madison Square Garden in New York City.

It is my understanding that the shows in England can be very large and extend over several days, with the Groups being scheduled on different days. I believe there is only one all-breed show in the U.S. that extends over two days, the Westminster Kennel Club Show. In our country we have cluster shows, where several different clubs will use the same show site over consecutive days.

Westminster Kennel Club is the oldest show in the US, and the entry is limited to 2500. In recent years, entry has been limited to Champions. This show is more formal than the majority of the shows with the judges wearing formal attire and the handlers fashionably dressed. In most instances the quality of the dogs is superb. After all, it is a show of Champions. It is a good show to study the AKC registered

Ch. Melody Lane Sings O' Al-Mar Luv gives judge Frank Oberstar a big kiss at the 1993 American Maltese Association National Specialty. breeds and is quite exciting—especially since it is televised. WKC is one of the few shows in this country that is still benched. This means the dog must be in his benched area during the show hours except when he is being groomed, in the ring, or being exercised.

Typically, the handlers are very particular about their appearances. They are careful not to wear something that will detract from their dog but will perhaps enhance it. American ring procedure is quite formal compared to that of other countries. Handlers should use discretion in the ring so as not to call attention to themselves. There is a certain etiquette expected between the judge and exhibitor and among the other exhibitors. Of course it is not always the case but the judge is supposed to be polite, not engaging in small talk or even acknowledging that he knows the handler. I understand that there is a more informal and relaxed atmosphere at the shows in other countries. For instance, the dress code is more casual. I can see where this might be more fun for the exhibitor and especially for the novice. This country is very handler-oriented in many of the breeds. It is true, in most instances, that the experienced professional handler can present the dog better and will have a feel for what a judge likes.

In England, Crufts is The Kennel Club's own show and is most assuredly the largest dog show in the world. They've been known to have an entry of nearly 20,000, and the show lasts four days. Entry is only gained by qualifying through winning in specified classes at another Championship Show. Westminster is strictly conformation, but Crufts exhibitors and spectators enjoy not only conformation but obedience, agility and a multitude of exhibitions as well. Obedience was admitted in 1957 and agility in 1983.

Ch. Shanlyn's Rais'n A Raucous has the poise and elegance that a Maltese needs to shine in the show ring.

If you are handling your own dog, please give some consideration to your apparel. For sure the dress code at

Henry says "thanks" to judge Robert Stein. A show Maltese is friendly and affectionate underneath his impeccably groomed "all business" exterior.

matches is more informal than the point shows. However, you should wear something a little more appropriate than beach attire or ragged jeans and bare feet. If you check out the handlers and see what is presently fashionable, you'll catch on. Men usually dress with a shirt and tie and a nice sports coat. Whether you are male or female, you will want to wear comfortable clothes and shoes. You need to be able to run with your dog and you certainly don't want to take a chance of falling and hurting yourself. Heaven forbid, if nothing else, you'll upset your dog. Women usually wear a dress or two-piece outfit, preferably with pockets to carry bait, comb, brush, etc. In this case men are the lucky ones with all their pockets. Ladies, think about where your dress will be if you need to kneel on the floor and also think about running. Does it allow freedom to do so?

Now it's time to pack for the show. You need to take along dog; crate; ex pen (if you use one); extra newspaper; water pail and water; all required grooming equipment, including hair dryer and extension cord; table; chair for you; bait for dog and lunch for you and friends; and, last but not least, clean up materials, such as plastic bags, paper towels, and perhaps a bath towel and some shampoo—just in case. Don't forget your entry confirmation and directions to the show.

If you are showing in obedience, then you will want to wear pants. Many of our top obedience handlers wear pants that are color-coordinated with their dogs. The philosophy is that imperfections in the black dog will be less obvious next to your black pants.

Whether you are showing in conformation, Junior Showmanship or obedience, you need to watch the clock and be sure you are not late. It is customary to pick up your conformation armband a few minutes before the start of the class. They will not wait for you and if you are on the show grounds and not in the ring, you will upset everyone. It's a little more complicated picking up your obedience armband if you show later in the class. If you have not picked up your armband and they get to your number, you may not be allowed to show. It's best to pick up your armband early, but then you may show earlier than expected if other handlers don't pick up. Customarily all conflicts should be discussed with the judge prior to the start of the class.

Junior Showmanship

The Junior Showmanship Class is a wonderful way to build self confidence even if there are no aspirations of staying with the dog-show game later in life. Frequently, Junior Showmanship becomes the background of those who become successful exhibitors/handlers in the future. In some instances it is taken very seriously, and success is measured in terms of wins. The Junior Handler is judged solely on his ability and skill in presenting his dog. The dog's conformation is not to be considered by the judge. Even so the condition and grooming of the dog may be a reflection upon the handler.

Usually the matches and point shows include different classes. The Junior Handler's dog may be entered in a breed or obedience class and even shown by another person in that class. Junior Showmanship classes are usually divided by age and perhaps sex. The age is determined by the handler's age on the day of the show. The classes are:

Novice Junior for those at least ten and under 14 years of age who at time of entry closing have not won three first places in a Novice Class at a licensed or member show.

Novice Senior for those at least 14 and under 18 years of age who at the time of entry closing have not won three first places in a Novice Class at a licensed or member show.

Vicki Abbott's daughter Tara, winning with her dog "Grammy." Tara was one of the top five Junior Handlers in the US in 1989, and she captured the Top Junior Toy Handler title.

Open Junior for those at least ten and under 14 years of age who at the time of entry closing have won at least three first places in a Novice Junior Showmanship Class at a licensed or member show with competition present.

Open Senior for those at least 14 and under 18 years of age who at

time of entry closing have won at least three first places in a Novice Junior Showmanship Class at a licensed or member show with competition present.

Junior Handlers must include their AKC Junior Handler number on each show entry. This needs to be obtained from the AKC.

CANINE GOOD CITIZEN

The AKC sponsors a program to encourage dog owners to train their dogs. Local clubs perform the pass/fail tests, and dogs who pass are awarded a Canine Good Citizen Certificate. Proof of vaccination is required at the time of participation. The test includes:

1. Accepting a friendly stranger.
2. Sitting politely for petting.
3. Appearance and grooming.
4. Walking on a loose leash.
5. Walking through a crowd.
6. Sit and down on command/staying in place.
7. Come when called.
8. Reaction to another dog.
9. Reactions to distractions.
10. Supervised separation.

If more effort was made by pet owners to accomplish these exercises, fewer dogs would be cast off to the humane shelter.

OBEDIENCE

Obedience is necessary, without a doubt, but it can also become a wonderful hobby or even an obsession. In my opinion, obedience classes and competition can provide wonderful companionship, not only with your dog but with your classmates or fellow competitors. It is always gratifying to

Breed judging at the 1992 Beverly Hills Kennel Club Show. Henry (far left) won Best of Breed and went on to win Group 1st.

discuss your dog's problems with others who have had similar experiences. The AKC acknowledged Obedience around 1936, and it has changed tremendously even though many of the exercises are basically the same. Today, obedience competition is just that—very competitive. Even so, it is possible for every obedience exhibitor to come home a winner (by earning qualifying scores) even though he/she may not earn a placement in the class.

Canine Good Citizen certification proves that your Maltese is as sweet as he looks.

Most of the obedience titles are awarded after earning three qualifying scores (legs) in the appropriate class under three different judges. These classes offer a perfect score of 200, which is extremely rare. Each of the class exercises has its own point value. A leg is earned after receiving a score of at least 170 and at least 50 percent of the points available in each exercise. The titles are:

Companion Dog—CD
This is called the Novice Class and the exercises are:

1. Heel on leash and figure 8	40 points
2. Stand for examination	30 points
3. Heel free	40 points
4. Recall	30 points
5. Long sit—one minute	30 points
6. Long down—three minutes	30 points
Maximum total score	200 points

Companion Dog Excellent—CDX
This is the Open Class and the exercises are:

1. Heel off leash and figure 8	40 points
2. Drop on recall	30 points
3. Retrieve on flat	20 points
4. Retrieve over high jump	30 points
5. Broad jump	20 points
6. Long sit—three minutes (out of sight)	30 points
7. Long down—five minutes (out of sight)	30 points
Maximum total score	200 points

Utility Dog—UD

The Utility Class exercises are:

1. Signal Exercise	40 points
2. Scent discrimination-Article 1	30 points
3. Scent discrimination-Article 2	30 points
4. Directed retrieve	30 points
5. Moving stand and examination	30 points
6. Directed jumping	40 points
Maximum total score	200 points

After achieving the UD title, you may feel inclined to go after the UDX and/or OTCh. The UDX (Utility Dog Excellent) title went into effect in January 1994. It is not easily attained. The title requires qualifying simultaneously ten times in Open B and Utility B but not necessarily at consecutive shows.

The OTCh (Obedience Trial Champion) is awarded after the dog has earned his UD and then goes on to earn 100 championship points, a first place in Utility, a first place in Open and another first place in either class. The placements must be won under three different judges at all-breed obedience trials. The points are determined by the number of dogs competing in the Open B and Utility B classes. The OTCh title precedes the dog's name.

Obedience matches (AKC Sanctioned, Fun, and Show and Go) are usually available. Usually they are sponsored by the local obedience clubs. When preparing an obedience dog for a title, you will find matches very helpful. Fun Matches and Show and Go Matches are more lenient in allowing you to make corrections in the ring. I frequently train (correct) in the ring and inform the judge that I would like to do so and to please mark me "exhibition." This means that I will not be eligible for any prize. This type of training is usually very

Pups destined for the show ring begin their preparation early in life. A young Maltese must learn to stand for examination and show off his best features.

Scylla's Electric Oops A Daisy, "Cookie," holds a CD title in obedience. She was bred by Larry and Vicki Abbott and is owner-handled by Lee Guzman.

necessary for the Open and Utility Classes. AKC Sanctioned Obedience Matches do not allow corrections in the ring since they must abide by the AKC Obedience Regulations. If you are interested in showing in obedience, then you should contact the AKC for a copy of the Obedience Regulations.

TRACKING

Tracking is officially classified obedience, but I feel it should have its own category. There are three tracking titles available: Tracking Dog (TD), Tracking Dog Excellent (TDX), Variable Surface Tracking (VST). If all three tracking titles are obtained, then the dog officially becomes a CT (Champion Tracker). The CT will go in front of the dog's name.

A TD may be earned anytime and does not have to follow the other obedience titles. There are many exhibitors that prefer tracking to obedience, and there are others like myself that do both. In my experience with small dogs, I prefer to earn the CD and CDX before attempting tracking. My reasoning is that small dogs are closer to the mat in the obedience rings and therefore it's too easy to put the nose down and sniff. Tracking encourages sniffing. Of course this depends on the dog. I've had some dogs that tracked around the ring and others (TDXs) who wouldn't think of sniffing in the ring.

AGILITY

Agility was first introduced by John Varley in England at the Crufts Dog Show, February 1978, but Peter Meanwell, competitor and judge, actually developed the idea. It was officially recognized in the early '80s. Agility is extremely popular in England and Canada and growing in popularity in the U.S. The AKC acknowledged agility in August 1994. Dogs must be at least 12 months of age to be entered. It is a fascinating sport that the dog, handler and spectators enjoy to the utmost. Agility is a spectator sport! The dog performs off lead. The handler either runs with his dog or positions himself on the course and directs his dog with verbal and hand signals over a timed course over or through a variety of obstacles including a time out or pause. One of the main drawbacks to agility is finding a place to train. The obstacles take up a lot of space and it is very time consuming to put up and take down courses.

The titles earned at AKC agility trials are Novice Agility Dog (NAD), Open Agility Dog (OAD), Agility Dog Excellent (ADX), and Master Agility Excellent (MAX). In order to acquire an agility title, a dog must earn a qualifying score in its respective class on three separate occasions under two different judges. The MAX will be awarded after earning ten qualifying scores in the Agility Excellent Class.

GENERAL INFORMATION

Obedience, tracking and agility allow the purebred dog with an Indefinite Listing Privilege (ILP) number or a limited registration to be exhibited and earn titles. Application must be made to the AKC for an ILP number.

The American Kennel Club publishes a monthly *Events* magazine that is part of the *Gazette*, their official journal for the sport of purebred dogs. The *Events* section lists upcoming shows and the secretary or superintendent for them. The majority of the conformation shows in the U.S. are overseen by licensed superintendents. Generally the entry closing date is approximately two-and-a-half weeks before the actual show. Point shows are fairly expensive, while the match shows cost about one third of the point show entry fee. Match shows usually take entries the day of the show but some are pre-entry. The best way to find match show information is through your local kennel club. Upon asking, the AKC can provide you with a list of superintendents, and you can write and ask to be put on their mailing lists.

Obedience trial and tracking test information is available through the AKC. Frequently these events are not superintended, but put on by the host club. Therefore you would make the entry with the event's secretary.

As you have read, there are numerous activities you can share with your dog. Regardless what you do, it does take teamwork. Your dog can only benefit from your attention and training. I hope this chapter has enlightened you and hope, if nothing else, you will attend a show here and there. Perhaps you will start with a puppy kindergarten class, and who knows where it may lead!

Ch. Scylla's Mina Maya Starfire was the top-winning Maltese of 1985. Bred, owned, and handled by Vicki Abbott.

HEALTH CARE

Veterinary medicine has become far more sophisticated than what was available to our ancestors. This can be attributed to the increase in household pets and consequently the demand for better care for them. Also human medicine has become far more complex. Today diagnostic testing in veterinary medicine parallels human diagnostics. Because of better technology we can expect our pets to live healthier lives thereby increasing their life spans.

THE FIRST CHECK UP

You will want to take your new puppy/dog in for its first check up within 48 to 72 hours after acquiring it. Many breeders strongly recommend this check up and so do the humane shelters. A puppy/dog can appear healthy but it may have a serious problem that is not apparent to the layman. Most pets have some type of a minor flaw that may never cause a real problem.

Puppies start out with an advantage in life if they come from two healthy parents who are free of hereditary disease and temperamentally sound.

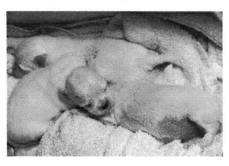

Unfortunately if he/she should have a serious problem, you will want to consider the consequences of keeping the pet and the attachments that will be formed, which may be broken prematurely. Keep in mind there are many healthy dogs looking for good homes.

This first check up is a good time to establish yourself with the veterinarian and learn the office policy regarding their hours and how they handle emergencies. Usually the breeder

Good health care will help your Maltese live longer. This Maltese is a senior citizen in the dog world—she's 15 years old!

or another conscientious pet owner is a good reference for locating a capable veterinarian. You should be aware that not all veterinarians give the same quality of service. Please do not make your selection on the least expensive clinic, as they may be short changing your pet. There is the possibility that eventually it will cost you more due to improper diagnosis, treatment, etc. If you are selecting a new veterinarian, feel free to ask for a tour of the clinic. You should inquire about making an appointment for a tour since all clinics are working clinics, and therefore may not be available all day for sightseers. You may worry less if you see where your pet will be spending the day if he ever needs to be hospitalized.

THE PHYSICAL EXAM

Your veterinarian will check your pet's overall condition, which includes listening to the heart; checking the respiration; feeling the abdomen, muscles and joints; checking the mouth, which includes the gum color and signs of gum disease along with plaque buildup; checking the ears for signs of an infection or ear mites; examining the eyes; and, last but not least, checking the condition of the skin and coat.

He should ask you questions regarding your pet's eating and elimination habits and invite you to relay your questions. It is a good idea to prepare a list so as not to forget anything. He should discuss the proper diet and the quantity to be fed. If this should differ from your breeder's recommendation, then you should convey to him the breeder's choice and see if he approves. If he recommends changing the diet, then this should be done over a few days so as not to cause a gastrointestinal upset. It is customary to take in a fresh stool sample (just a small amount) for a test for intestinal parasites. It must be fresh, preferably within 12 hours, since the eggs hatch quickly and after hatching will not be observed under the microscope. If your pet isn't obliging then, usually the technician can take one in the clinic.

IMMUNIZATIONS

It is important that you take your puppy/dog's vaccination record with you on your first visit. In case of a puppy, presumably the breeder has seen to the vaccinations up to the time you acquired custody. Veterinarians differ in their vaccination protocol. It is not unusual for your puppy to have received vaccinations for distemper, hepatitis, leptospirosis, parvovirus and parainfluenza every four to six weeks from the age of six to eight weeks. Usually this is a combined injection and is typically called the DHLPP. The DHLPP is given through at least 16 weeks of age, and it is customary to continue with another parvovirus vaccine at 16 to 18 weeks. Leptospirosis vaccine can be the cause of anaphylactic reactions in toy breeds. Since this vaccine is only recommended in at-risk cases and its duration of immunity is poor, we eliminate it from the vaccine. You may wonder why so many immunizations are necessary. No one knows for sure when the puppy's maternal antibodies are gone, although it is customarily accepted that distemper antibodies are gone by 12 weeks. Usually parvovirus antibodies are gone by 16 to 18 weeks of age. However, it is possible for the maternal antibodies to be gone at a much earlier age or even a later age. Therefore immunizations are started at an early age. The vaccine will not give immunity as long as there are maternal antibodies.

The rabies vaccination is given at six months or older depending on your local laws. A vaccine for bordetella (kennel cough) is advisable and can be given anytime from the age of six weeks. The coronavirus is not commonly given unless there is a problem locally. The Lyme vaccine is necessary in endemic areas. Lyme disease has been reported in 47 states.

Distemper

This is virtually an incurable disease. If the dog recovers, he is subject to severe nervous disorders. The virus attacks every tissue in the body and resembles a bad cold with a fever. It can cause a runny nose and eyes and cause gastrointestinal disorders, including a poor appetite, vomiting and diarrhea.

The most important preventive health measure you can take with your new puppy is to make sure that he is properly vaccinated.

The virus is carried by raccoons, foxes, wolves, mink and other dogs. Unvaccinated youngsters and senior citizens are very susceptible. This is still a common disease.

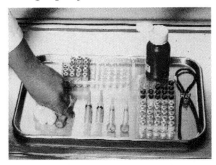

Hepatitis

This is a virus that is most serious in very young dogs. It is spread by contact with an infected animal or its stool or urine. The virus affects the liver and kidneys and is characterized by high fever, depression and lack of appetite. Recovered animals may be afflicted with chronic illnesses. This disease is now considered extremely rare.

Leptospirosis

This is a bacterial disease transmitted by contact with the urine of an infected dog, rat or other wildlife. It produces severe symptoms of fever, depression, jaundice and internal bleeding and was fatal before the vaccine was developed. Recovered dogs can be carriers, and the disease can be transmitted from dogs to humans. Most vets only recommend this vaccine to toy dogs at risk.

Parvovirus

This was first noted in the late 1970s and is still a fatal disease. However, with proper vaccinations, early diagnosis and prompt treatment, it is a manageable disease. It attacks the bone marrow and intestinal tract. The symptoms include depression, loss of appetite, vomiting, diarrhea and collapse. Immediate medical attention is of the essence. It has been noted that high doses of vitamin C are effective in the treatment of parvovirus.

Rabies

This is shed in the saliva and is carried by raccoons, skunks, foxes, other dogs and cats. It attacks nerve tissue, resulting in paralysis and death. Rabies can be transmitted to people and is virtually always fatal. This disease is reappearing in the suburbs.

Bordetella (Kennel Cough)

The symptoms are coughing, sneezing, hacking and retching accompanied by nasal discharge usually lasting from a few days to several weeks. There are several disease-producing organisms responsible for this disease. The

Dogs that are kept together in close quarters run a higher risk of kennel cough, which is highly contagious. Have your Maltese vaccinated to greatly reduce the risk.

present vaccines are helpful but do not protect for all the strains. It usually is not life threatening but in some instances it can progress to a serious bronchopneumonia. The disease is highly contagious. The vaccination should be given routinely for dogs that come in contact with other dogs, such as through boarding, training class or visits to the groomer.

Coronavirus

This is usually self limiting and not life threatening. It was first noted in the late '70s about a year before parvovirus. The virus produces a yellow/brown stool and there may be depression, vomiting and diarrhea.

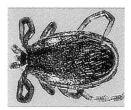

The deer tick is the most common carrier of Lyme disease. Photo courtesy of Virbac Laboratories, Inc., Fort Worth, Texas.

Lyme Disease

This was first diagnosed in the United States in 1976 in Lyme, CT in people who lived in close proximity to the deer tick. Symptoms may include acute lameness, fever, swelling of joints and loss of appetite. Your veterinarian can advise you if you live in an endemic area.

After your puppy has completed his puppy vaccinations, you will continue to booster as often as is recommended, either by the breeder or your veterinarian. Rabies boosters depend on your local law.

Annual Visit

I would like to impress the importance of the annual check up, which would include possible booster vaccinations, check for intestinal parasites and test for heartworm. Today in our very busy world it is rush, rush and see "how much you can get for how little." Unbelievably, some non-veterinary businesses have entered into the vaccination business. More harm than good can come to your dog through improper vaccinations, possibly from inferior vaccines and/or the wrong schedule. More than likely you truly care about your companion dog and over the years you have devoted much time and expense to his well being. Perhaps you are unaware that a vaccination is not just a vaccination. There is more

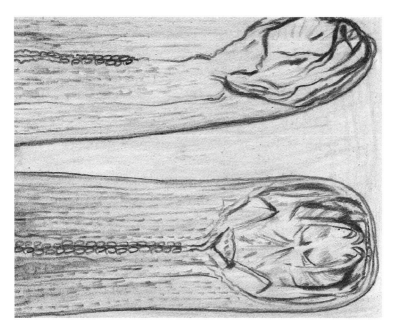

Hookworms are almost microscopic intestinal worms that can cause anemia and therefore serious problems, even death.

involved. Many toy dogs may have allergic, or anaphylactic, reactions to vaccines. Please, please follow through with regular physical examinations. It is so important for your veterinarian to know your dog and this is especially true during middle age through the geriatric years. More than likely your older dog will require more than one physical a year. The annual physical is good preventive medicine. Through early diagnosis and subsequent treatment your dog can maintain a longer and better quality of life.

INTESTINAL PARASITES

Hookworms

These are almost microscopic intestinal worms that can cause anemia and therefore serious problems, including death, in young puppies. Hookworms can be transmitted to humans through penetration of the skin. Puppies may be born with them.

Roundworms

These are spaghetti-like worms that can cause a potbellied appearance and dull coat along with more severe symptoms, such as vomiting, diarrhea and coughing. Puppies acquire these while in the mother's uterus and through lactation. Both hookworms and roundworms may be acquired through ingestion.

Whipworms

These have a three-month life cycle and are not acquired through the dam. They cause intermittent diarrhea usually with mucus. Whipworms are possibly the most difficult worm to eradicate. Their eggs are very resistant to most environmental factors and can last for years until the proper conditions enable them to mature. Whipworms are seldom seen in the stool.

Whipworms are hard to find unless one strains the feces, and that is best left to a veterinarian. Pictured here are adult whipworms.

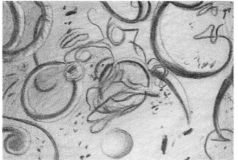

Intestinal parasites are more prevalent in some areas than others. Climate, soil and contamination are big factors contributing to the incidence of intestinal parasites. Eggs are passed in the stool, lay on the ground and then become infective in a certain number of days. Each of the above worms has a different life cycle.

Your best chance of becoming and remaining worm-free is to always pooper-scoop your yard. A fenced-in yard keeps stray dogs out, which is certainly helpful.

I would recommend having a fecal examination on your dog twice a year or more often if there is a problem. If your dog has a positive fecal sample, then he will be given the appropriate medication and you will be asked to bring back another stool sample in a certain period of time (depending on the type of worm) and then be rewormed. This process goes on until he has at least two negative samples. The different types of worms require different medications. You will be wasting your money and doing your dog an injustice by buying over-the-counter medication without first consulting your veterinarian.

OTHER INTERNAL PARASITES

Coccidiosis and Giardiasis

These protozoal infections usually affect puppies, especially in places where large numbers of puppies are brought together. Older dogs may harbor these infections but do not show signs unless they are stressed. Symptoms include diarrhea, weight loss and lack of appetite. These infections are not always apparent in the fecal examination.

Tapeworms

Seldom apparent on fecal floatation, they are diagnosed frequently as rice-like segments around the dog's anus and the base of the tail. Tapeworms are long, flat and ribbon like, sometimes several feet in length, and made up of many segments about five-eighths of an inch long. The two most common ways your dog can acquire tapeworms are:

(1) First the larval form of the flea tapeworm parasite must mature in an intermediate host, the flea, before it can become infective. Your dog acquires this by ingesting the flea through licking and chewing.

(2) Rabbits, rodents and certain large game animals serve as intermediate hosts for other species of tapeworms. If your dog should eat one of these infected hosts, then he can acquire tapeworms.

Certain diseases can be especially dangerous to young puppies, which is why receiving the right vaccinations at the right age is such a necessity.

Heartworm Disease

This is a worm that resides in the heart and adjacent blood vessels of the lung that produces microfilaria, which circulate in the bloodstream. It is possible for a dog to be infected with any number of worms from one to a hundred that can be 6 to 14 inches long. It is a life-threatening disease, expensive to treat and easily prevented. Depending on where you live, your veterinarian may recommend a preventive year-round and either an annual or semiannual blood test. The most common preventive is given once a month.

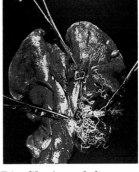

Dirofilaria—adult worms in the heart of a dog. It is possible for a dog to be infected with any number of worms that can be 6 to 14 inches long. Courtesy of Merck AgVet.

External Parasites

Fleas

These pests are not only the dog's worst enemy but also enemy to the owner's pocketbook. Preventing is less expensive than treating, but regardless I think we'd prefer to spend our money elsewhere. I would guess that the majority of our dogs are allergic to the bite of a flea, and in many cases it only takes one flea bite. The protein in the flea's saliva is the culprit. Allergic dogs have a reaction, which usually results in a "hot spot." More than likely such a reaction will involve a trip to the veterinarian for treatment. Yes, prevention is less expensive. Fortunately today there are several good products available.

If there is a flea infestation, no one product is going to correct the problem. Not only will the dog require treatment so will the environment. In general flea collars are not very effective although there is now available an "egg" collar that will kill the eggs on the dog. Dips are the most economical but they are messy. There are some effective shampoos and treatments available through pet shops and veterinarians. An oral tablet arrived on the American market in 1995 and was popular in Europe the previous year. It sterilizes the female flea but will not kill adult fleas. Therefore the tablet, which is given monthly, will decrease the flea population but is not a "cure-all." Those dogs that suffer from flea-bite allergy will still be subjected to the bite of the flea. Another popular parasiticide is permethrin, which is applied to the back of the dog in one or two places depending on the dog's weight. This product works as a repellent causing the flea to get "hot feet" and jump off. Do not confuse this product with some of the organophosphates that are also applied to the dog's back.

Some products are not usable on young puppies. Treating fleas should be done under your veterinarian's guidance. Frequently it is necessary to combine products and the layman does not have the knowledge regarding possible toxicities. It is hard to believe but there are a few dogs that do have a natural resistance to fleas. Nevertheless it would be wise to treat all pets at the same time. Don't forget your cats. Cats just love to prowl the neighborhood and consequently return with unwanted guests.

Adult fleas live on the dog but their eggs drop off the dog into the environment. There they go through four larval stages before reaching adulthood, and thereby are able to jump back on the poor unsuspecting dog. The cycle resumes and takes between 21 to 28 days under ideal conditions. There are environmental products available that will kill both the adult fleas and the larvae.

Ticks

Ticks carry Rocky Mountain Spotted Fever, Lyme disease and can cause tick paralysis. They should be removed with tweezers, trying to pull out the head. The jaws carry disease.

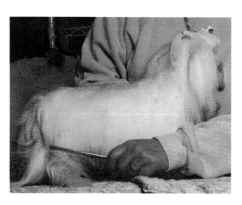

There is a tick preventive collar that does an excellent job. The ticks automatically back out on those dogs wearing collars.

Regularly grooming your Maltese will help you detect any signs of parasite infestation or other skin problems.

To prevent and eliminate flea infestation in the house, use a safe insecticide to kill adult fleas, and treat the environment with an insect growth regulator to stop eggs and larvae.

Sarcoptic Mange

This is a mite that is difficult to find on skin scrapings. Sarcoptes are highly contagious to other dogs and to humans although they do not live long on humans. They cause intense itching. Sarcoptic mites are usually found on the skin of the ears, elbows, legs and face. Hair loss, red bumps and crusty skin are indications.

Demodectic Mange

This is a mite that is passed from the dam to her puppies. It affects dogs up to one year of age. Diagnosis is confirmed by skin scraping. Small areas hair loss (giving a moth-eaten look) around the eyes, lips and/or forelegs become visible. There is little itching unless there is a secondary bacterial infection. Some breeds are afflicted more than others.

Cheyletiella Mange

This causes intense itching and is diagnosed by skin scraping. It lives in the outer layers of the skin of dogs, cats, rabbits and humans. Yellow-gray scales, appearing like heavy dandruff, may be found on the back and the rump, top of the head and the nose. For all types of mange, consult your veterinarian for treatment.

To Breed or Not To Breed

More than likely your breeder has requested that you have your puppy neutered or spayed. Your breeder's request is based on what is healthiest for your dog and what is most beneficial for your breed. Experienced and conscientious breeders devote many years into developing a bloodline. In order to do this, he makes every effort to plan each breeding in regard to conformation, temperament and health. This type of breeder does his best to perform the necessary testing (i.e., OFA, CERF, testing for inherited blood disorders, thyroid, etc.). Testing is expensive and sometimes very disheartening when a favorite dog doesn't pass his health tests. The health history pertains not only to the breeding stock but to the immediate ancestors. Reputable breeders do not want their offspring to be bred indiscriminately. Therefore you may be asked to neuter or spay your puppy. Of course there is always the exception, and your breeder may agree to let you breed your dog under his direct supervision. This is an important concept. More and more effort is being made to breed healthier dogs.

Spay/Neuter

There are numerous benefits of performing this surgery at six months of age. Unspayed females are subject to mammary and ovarian cancer. Later in life, an unspayed female may develop a pyometra (an infected uterus), which is definitely life threatening.

Spaying is performed under a general anesthetic and is easy on the young dog. As you might expect it is a little harder on the older dog, but that is no reason to deny her the surgery. The surgery removes the ovaries and uterus.

Neutering the male at a young age will inhibit some characteristic male behavior that owners frown upon. I have found my boys will not hike their legs and mark territory if they are neutered at six months of age. Also neutering at a young age has hormonal benefits, lessening the chance of hormonal aggressiveness.

Surgery involves removing the testicles but leaving the scrotum. If there should be a retained testicle, then he definitely needs to be neutered before the age of two or three years. Retained testicles can develop into cancer. Unneutered males are at risk for testicular cancer, perineal fistulas, perianal tumors and fistulas and prostatic disease.

Intact males and females are prone to housebreaking accidents. Females urinate frequently before, during and after heat cycles, and males tend to mark territory if there is a female in heat. Males may show the same behavior if there is a visiting dog or guests.

All Maltese puppies are adorable, but not all are of breeding quality. Many breeders sell pet puppies under the condition that the new owners have the pups spayed or neutered.

Surgery involves a sterile operating procedure equivalent to human surgery. The incision site is shaved, surgically scrubbed and draped. The veterinarian wears a sterile surgical gown, cap, mask and gloves. Anesthesia should be monitored by a registered technician. It is customary for the veterinarian to recommend a pre-anesthetic blood screening, looking

for metabolic problems and a ECG rhythm strip to check for normal heart function. Today anesthetics are equal to human anesthetics, which enables your dog to walk out of the clinic the same day as surgery.

Some folks worry about their dog gaining weight after being neutered or spayed. This is usually not the case. It is true that some dogs may be less active so they could develop a problem, but my own dogs are just as active as they were before surgery. However, if your dog should begin to gain, then you need to decrease his food and see to it that he gets a little more exercise.

DENTAL CARE for Your Dog's Life

So you've got a new puppy! You also have a new set of puppy teeth in your household. Anyone who has ever raised a puppy is abundantly aware of these new teeth. Your puppy will chew anything it can reach, chase your shoelaces, and play "tear the rag" with any piece of clothing it can find. When puppies are newly born, they have no teeth. At about four weeks of age, puppies of most breeds begin to develop their deciduous or baby teeth. They begin eating semi-solid food, fighting and biting with their litter mates, and learning discipline from their mother. As their new teeth come in, they inflict more pain on their mother's breasts, so her feeding sessions become less frequent and shorter. By six or eight weeks, the mother will start growling to warn her pups when they are fighting too roughly or hurting her as they nurse too much with their new teeth.

All of Nylabone®'s tempting toys come in different sizes for different-sized dogs. The petite size is just right for these Maltese puppies.

Puppies need to chew. It is a necessary part of their physical and mental development. They develop muscles and necessary life skills as they drag objects around, fight over possession, and vocalize alerts and warnings. Puppies chew on things to explore their world. They are using their sense of taste to determine what is food and what is not. How else can they tell

Your Maltese will be happier and his teeth and gums healthier if you give him a POPpup™ to chew on. Every POPpup™ is 100% edible and enhanced with dog-friendly ingredients like liver, cheese, spinach, chicken, carrots or potatoes. What you won't find in a POPpup™ is salt, sugar, alcohol, plastic or preservatives. You can even microwave a POPpup™ to turn it into a huge crackly treat for your Maltese to enjoy. Available at your local pet shop.

an electrical cord from a lizard? At about four months of age, most puppies begin shedding their baby teeth. Often these teeth need some help to come out and make way for the permanent teeth. The incisors (front teeth) will be replaced first. Then, the adult canine or fang teeth erupt. When the baby tooth is not shed before the permanent tooth comes in, veterinarians call it a retained deciduous tooth. This condition will often cause gum infections by trapping hair and debris between the permanent tooth and the retained baby tooth. Nylafloss® is an excellent device for puppies to use. They can toss it, drag it, and chew on the many surfaces it presents. The baby teeth can catch in the nylon material, aiding in their removal. Puppies that have adequate chew toys will have less destructive behavior, develop more physically, and have less chance of retained deciduous teeth.

During the first year, your dog should be seen by your veterinarian at regular intervals. Your veterinarian will let you know when to bring in your puppy for vaccinations and parasite examinations. At each visit, your veterinarian should inspect the lips, teeth, and mouth as part of a complete physical examination. You should take some part in the maintenance of your dog's oral health. You should examine your dog's mouth weekly throughout his first year to make sure there are no sores, foreign objects, tooth problems, etc. If your dog drools excessively, shakes its head, or has bad breath, consult your veterinarian. By the time your dog is six months old, the permanent teeth are all in and plaque can start to accumulate on the tooth surfaces. This is when your dog needs to develop good dental-care habits to prevent calculus build-up on its teeth. Brushing is best. That is a fact that cannot be denied. However, some dogs do not like their teeth brushed regularly, or you may not be able to accomplish the task. In that case, you should consider a product that will help prevent plaque and calculus build-up.

The Plaque Attackers® and Galileo Bone® are other excellent choices for the first three years of a dog's life. Their shapes make them interesting for the dog. As the dog chews on them, the solid polyurethane massages the gums which improves the blood circulation to the periodontal tissues. Projections on the chew devices increase the surface and are in contact with the tooth for more efficient cleaning. The unique shape and consistency prevent your dog from exerting excessive force on his own teeth or from breaking off pieces of the bone. If your dog is an aggressive chewer or weighs more than 55 pounds

Gumabones® are made of non-toxic, durable polyurethane that is great for smaller dogs and less aggressive chewers. There are even chicken and liver flavored Gumabones® to satisfy your Maltese's mouth and nose. Available at your local pet shop.

(25 kg), you should consider giving him a Nylabone®, the most durable chew product on the market.

The Gumabone®, made by the Nylabone Company, is constructed of strong polyurethane, which is softer than nylon. Less powerful chewers prefer the Gumabones® to the Nylabones®. A super option for your dog is the Hercules Bone®, a uniquely shaped bone named after the great Olympian for its exceptional strength. Like all Nylabone products, they are specially scented to make them attractive to your dog. Ask

Dogs become quite attached to their favorite toys. This Maltese pup has a hold on his Gumabone® that says, "I'm not sharing!"

During your Maltese's annual veterinary visit, his mouth, teeth, lips, and gums will be examined. Regular maintenance on your part will help protect against periodontal disease.

your veterinarian about these bones and he will validate the good doctor's prescription: Nylabones® not only give your dog a good chewing workout but also help to save your dog's teeth (and

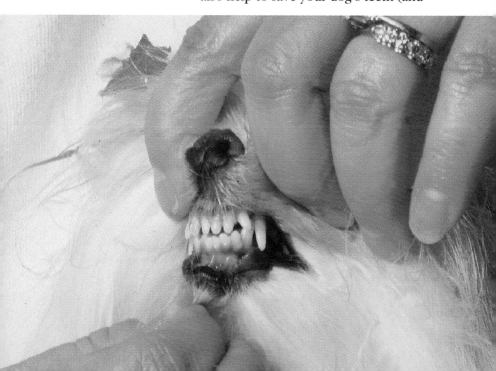

even his life, as it protects him from possible fatal periodontal diseases).

By the time dogs are four years old, 75% of them have periodontal disease. It is the most common infection in dogs. Yearly examinations by your veterinarian are essential to maintaining your dog's good health. If your veterinarian detects periodontal disease, he or she may recommend a prophylactic cleaning. To do a thorough cleaning, it will be necessary to put your dog under anesthesia. With modern gas anesthetics and monitoring equipment, the procedure is pretty safe. Your veterinarian will scale the teeth with an ultrasound scaler or hand instrument. This removes the calculus from the teeth. If there are calculus deposits below the gum line, the veterinarian will plane the roots to make them smooth. After all of the calculus has been removed, the teeth are polished with pumice in a polishing cup. If any medical or surgical treatment is needed, it is done at this time. The final step would be fluoride treatment and your follow-up treatment at home. If the periodontal disease is advanced, the veterinarian may prescribe a medicated mouth rinse or antibiotics for use at home. Make sure your dog has safe, clean and attractive chew toys and treats. Chooz® treats are another way of using a consumable treat to help keep your dog's teeth clean.

Rawhide is the most popular of all materials for a dog to chew. This has never been good news to dog owners, because rawhide is inherently very dangerous for dogs. Thousands of dogs have died from rawhide, having swallowed the hide after it has become soft and mushy, only to cause stomach and intestinal blockage. A new rawhide product on the market has finally solved the problem of rawhide: molded Roar-Hide® from Nylabone. These are composed of processed, cut up, and melted American rawhide injected into your dog's favorite shape: a dog bone. These dog-safe devices smell and taste like rawhide but don't break up. The ridges on the bones help to fight tartar build-up on the teeth and they last ten times longer than the usual rawhide chews.

As your dog ages, professional examination and cleaning should become more frequent. The mouth should be inspected at least once a year. Your veterinarian may recommend visits every six months. In the geriatric patient, organs such as the heart, liver, and kidneys do not function as well as when they were young. Your veterinarian will probably want to test these organs' functions prior to using general anesthesia for dental cleaning. If your dog is a good chewer and you work closely with your veterinarian, your dog can keep all of its teeth all of its life. However, as your dog ages, his sense of smell, sight, and taste will diminish. He may not have the desire to chase, trap or chew his toys. He will also not have the energy to chew for long periods, as arthritis and periodontal disease make chewing painful. This will leave you with more responsibility for keeping his teeth clean and healthy. The dog that would not let you brush his teeth at one year of age, may let you brush his teeth now that he is ten years old.

To combat boredom and relieve your Maltese's natural desire to chew, there's nothing better than a Roar-Hide™. Unlike common rawhide, this bone won't turn into a gooey mess when chewed on, so your dog won't choke on small pieces of it, and your carpet won't be stained by it. The Roar-Hide™ is completely edible and is high in protein (over 86%) and low in fat (less than 1/3 of 1%). The regular-sized Roar-Hide™ is just right for your Maltese. Available at your local pet shop.

If you train your dog with good chewing habits as a puppy, he will have healthier teeth throughout his life.

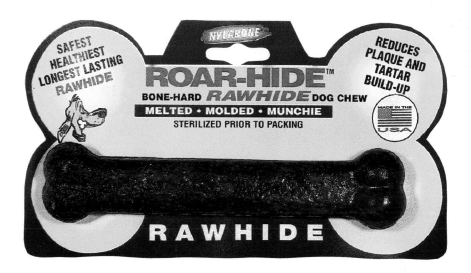

IDENTIFICATION and Finding the Lost Dog

There are several ways of identifying your dog. The old standby is a collar with dog license, rabies, and ID tags. Unfortunately collars have a way of being separated from the dog and tags fall off. I am not suggesting you shouldn't use a collar and tags. If they stay intact and on the dog, they are the quickest way of identification.

For several years owners have been tattooing their dogs. Some tattoos use a number with a registry. Here lies the problem because there are several registries to check. If you wish to tattoo, use your social security number. The humane shelters have the means to trace it. It is usually done on the inside of the rear thigh. The area is first shaved and numbed. There is no pain, although a few dogs do not like the buzzing sound. Occasionally tattooing is not legible and needs to be redone.

The newest method of identification is microchipping. The microchip is a computer chip that is no larger than a grain of rice. The veterinarian implants it by injection between the shoulder blades. The dog feels no discomfort. If your dog is lost and picked up by the humane society, they can trace you by scanning the microchip, which has its own code. Microchip scanners are friendly to other brands of microchips and their registries. The microchip comes with a dog tag saying the dog is microchipped. It is the safest way of identifying your dog.

FINDING THE LOST DOG

I am sure you will agree with me that there would be little worse than losing your dog. Responsible pet owners rarely lose their dogs. They do not let their dogs run free because they don't want harm to come to them. Not only that but in most, if not all, states there is a leash law.

Beware of fenced-in yards. They can be a hazard. Dogs find ways to escape either over or under the fence. Another fast exit is through the gate that perhaps the neighbor's child left unlocked.

Below is a list that hopefully will be of help to you if you need it. Remember don't give up, keep looking. Your dog is worth your efforts.

1. Contact your neighbors and put flyers with a photo on it in their mailboxes. Information you should include would be the dog's name, breed, sex, color, age, source of identification, when your dog was last seen and where, and your name and phone numbers. It may be helpful to say the dog needs medical care. Offer a *reward*.

2. Check all local shelters daily. It is also possible for your dog to be picked up away from home and end up in an out-of-the-way shelter. Check these too. Go in person. It is not good enough to call. Most shelters are limited on the time they can hold dogs then they are put up for adoption or euthanized. There is the possibility that your dog will not make it to the shelter for several days. Your dog could have been wandering or someone may have tried to keep him.

The newest method of identification is microchipping. The microchip is a computer chip that is no bigger than a grain of rice.

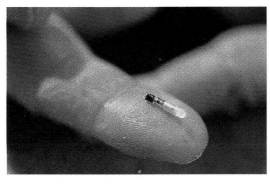

3. Notify all local veterinarians. Call and send flyers.

4. Call your breeder. Frequently breeders are contacted when one of their breed is found.

5. Contact the rescue group for your breed.

6. Contact local schools—children may have seen your dog.

7. Post flyers at the schools, groceries, gas stations, convenience stores, veterinary clinics, groomers and any other place that will allow them.

8. Advertise in the newspaper.

9. Advertise on the radio.

TRAVELING with Your Dog

The earlier you start traveling with your new puppy or dog, the better. He needs to become accustomed to traveling. However, some dogs are nervous riders and become carsick easily. It is helpful if he starts with an empty stomach. Do not despair, as it will go better if you continue taking him with you on short fun rides. How would you feel if every time you rode in the car you stopped at the doctor's for an injection? You would soon dread that nasty car. Older dogs that tend to get carsick may have more of a problem adjusting to traveling. Those dogs that are having a serious problem may benefit from some medication prescribed by the veterinarian.

Do give your dog a chance to relieve himself before getting into the car. It is a good idea to be prepared for a clean up with a leash, paper towels, bag and terry cloth towel.

The safest place for your dog is in a fiberglass crate, although close confinement can promote carsickness in some dogs. If your dog is nervous you can try letting him ride on the seat next to you or in someone's lap.

An alternative to the crate would be to use a car harness made for dogs and/or a safety strap attached to the harness or

"Wait for me!" Some Maltese are content to stay at home, while others are more anxious to get out and see the world.

Crates are a safe way for your dog to travel. The fiberglass crates are safest but the metal crates allow more air.

collar. Whatever you do, do not let your dog ride in the back of a pickup truck. I've seen trucks stop quickly and, even though the dog was tied, it fell out and was dragged.

I do occasionally let my dogs ride loose with me because I really enjoy their companionship, but in all honesty they are safer in their crates. I have a friend whose van rolled in an accident but his dogs, in their fiberglass crates, were not injured nor did they escape. However, it is not a good idea to leave a crated dog alone in a car. Keep in mind that while many dogs are overly protective in their crates, this may not be enough to deter dognappers. In some states it is against the law to leave a dog in the car unattended.

Never leave a dog loose in the car wearing a collar and leash. I have known more than one dog that has killed himself by hanging. Do not let him put his head out an open window. Foreign debris can be blown into his eyes. When leaving your dog unattended in a car, consider the temperature. It can take less than five minutes to reach temperatures over 100 degrees Fahrenheit.

TRIPS

Perhaps you are taking a trip. Give consideration to what is best for your dog—traveling with you or boarding. When traveling by car, van or motor home, you need to think ahead about locking your vehicle. In all probability you have many valuables in the car and do not wish to leave it unlocked. Perhaps most valuable and not replaceable is your dog. Give thought to securing your vehicle and providing adequate ventilation for him. Another consideration for you when traveling with your dog is medical problems that may arise and little inconveniences, such as exposure to external parasites. Some areas of the country are quite flea infested. You may want to carry flea spray with you. This is even a good idea when staying in motels. Quite possibly you are not the only occupant of the room.

The safest way to transport several dogs is to have them secure in their individual crates.

Unbelievably many motels and even hotels do allow canine guests, even some very first-class ones. Gaines Pet Foods Corporation publishes *Touring With Towser*, a directory of domestic hotels and motels that accommodate guests with dogs. Their address is Gaines TWT, PO Box 5700, Kankakee, IL, 60902. I would recommend you call ahead to any motel that you may be considering and see if they accept pets. Sometimes it is necessary to pay a deposit against room damage. Of course you are more likely to gain accommodations for a small dog than a large dog. Also the management feels reassured when you mention that your dog will be crated. Since my dogs tend to bark when I leave the room, I leave the TV on nearly full blast to deaden the noises outside that tend to encourage my dogs to bark. If you do travel with your dog, take along plenty of baggies so that you can clean up after him. When we all do our share in cleaning up, we make it possible for motels to continue accepting our pets. As a matter of fact, you should practice cleaning up everywhere you take your dog.

Depending on where your are traveling, you may need an up-to-date health certificate issued by your veterinarian. It is good policy to take along your dog's medical information, which would include the name, address and phone number of

your veterinarian, vaccination record, rabies certificate, and any medication he is taking.

AIR TRAVEL

When traveling by air, you need to contact the airlines to check their policy. Usually you have to make arrangements up to a couple of weeks in advance for traveling with your dog. The airlines require your dog to travel in an airline approved fiberglass crate. Usually these can be purchased through the airlines but they are also readily available in most pet-supply stores. If your dog is not accustomed to a crate, then it is a good idea to get him acclimated to it before your trip. The day of the actual trip you should withhold water about one hour ahead of departure and no food for about 12 hours. The airlines generally have temperature restrictions, which do not allow pets to travel if it is either too cold or too hot. Frequently these restrictions are based on the temperatures at the departure and arrival airports. It's best to inquire about a health certificate. These usually need to be issued within ten days of departure. You should arrange for non-stop, direct flights and if a commuter plane should be involved, check to see if it will carry dogs. Some don't. The Humane Society of the United States has put together a tip sheet for airline traveling. You can receive a copy by sending a self-addressed stamped envelope to:

If your Maltese is going to accompany you on trip by airplane, you will have to purchase an approved fiberglass crate for him to travel in.

The Humane Society of the United States
Tip Sheet
2100 L Street NW
Washington, DC 20037.

Although fiberglass crates are safer for traveling, wire crates are often preferred for boarding because they let in more air and allow the dog to see more of his surroundings.

A portable exercise pen can be easily brought with you on a trip to give your Maltese a safe place to play once you reach your destination.

Regulations differ for traveling outside of the country and are sometimes changed without notice. Well in advance you need to write or call the appropriate consulate or agricultural department for instructions. Some countries have lengthy quarantines (six months), and countries differ in their rabies vaccination requirements. For instance, it may have to be given at least 30 days ahead of your departure.

Do make sure your dog is wearing proper identification. You never know when you might be in an accident and separated from your dog. Or your dog could be frightened and somehow manage to escape and run away. When traveling, it is a good idea for your dogs to wear collars with engraved nameplates with your name, phone number and city.

Another suggestion would be to carry in-case-of-emergency instructions. These would include the address and phone number of a relative or friend, your veterinarian's name, address and phone number, and your dog's medical information.

BOARDING KENNELS

Perhaps you have decided that you need to board your dog. Your veterinarian can recommend a good boarding facility or possibly a pet sitter that will come to your house. It is customary for the boarding kennel to ask for proof of vaccination for the DHLPP, rabies and bordetella vaccine. The bordetella should have been given within six months of boarding. This is for your protection. If they do not ask for this proof I would not board at their kennel. Ask about flea control. Those dogs that suffer flea-bite allergy can get in trouble at a boarding kennel. Unfortunately boarding kennels are limited on how much they are able to do.

A reputable boarding kennel will require that dogs receive the vaccination for kennel cough no later than two weeks before their scheduled stay.

For more information on pet sitting, contact NAPPS: National Association of Professional Pet Sitters 1200 G Street, NW Suite 760 Washington, DC 20005.

Some clinics have technicians that pet sit and technicians that board clinic patients in their homes. This may be an alternative for you. Ask your veterinarian if they have an employee that can help you. There is a definite advantage of having a technician care for your dog, especially if your dog is on medication or is a senior citizen.

You can write for a copy of *Traveling With Your Pet* from ASPCA, Education Department, 441 E. 92nd Street, New York, NY 10128.

BEHAVIOR and Canine Communication

Studies of the human/animal bond point out the importance of the unique relationships that exist between people and their pets. Those of us who share our lives with pets understand the special part they play through companionship, service and protection. For many, the pet/owner bond goes beyond simple companionship; pets are often considered members of the family. A leading pet food manufacturer recently conducted a nationwide survey of pet owners to gauge just how important pets were in their lives. Here's what they found:

An affinity for the Maltese must run in the family—this is Vicki Abbott's daughter Aubrey with two nephews of the famous Ch. Sand Island Small Kraft Lite.

- 76 percent allow their pets to sleep on their beds
- 78 percent think of their pets as their children
- 84 percent display photos of their pets, mostly in their homes.
- 100 percent talk to their pets
- 97 percent think that their pets understand what they're saying

Are you surprised?

Senior citizens show more concern for their own eating habits when they have the responsibility of feeding a dog. Seeing that their dog is routinely exercised encourages the owner to think of schedules that otherwise may seem unimportant to the senior citizen. The older owner may be arthritic and feeling poorly but with responsibility for his dog he has a reason to get up and get moving. It is a big plus if his dog is an attention seeker who will demand such from his owner.

Over the last couple of decades, it has been shown that pets relieve the stress of those who lead busy lives. Owning a pet has been known to lessen the occurrence of heart attack and stroke.

Many single folks thrive on the companionship of a dog. Lifestyles are very different from a long time ago, and today more individuals seek the single life. However, they receive fulfillment from owning a dog.

Most likely the majority of our dogs live in family environments. The companionship they provide is well worth the effort involved. In my opinion, every child should have the opportunity to have a family dog. Dogs teach responsibility through understanding their care, feelings and even respecting their life cycles. Frequently those children who have not been exposed to dogs grow up afraid of dogs, which isn't good. Dogs sense timidity and some will take advantage of the situation.

Today more dogs are serving as service dogs. Since the origination of the Seeing Eye dogs years ago, we now have trained hearing dogs. Also dogs are trained to provide service for the handicapped and are able to perform many different tasks for their owners. Search and Rescue dogs,

Multiple Best in Show winner Ch. Shanlyn's Rais'n A Raucous is used to being in the spotlight.

Scylla's Jo-Li Lite My Fire, "Willy," is a Hearing Impaired Training Dog who is indispensable to his owner, Rosemarie Saccardi.

with their handlers, are sent throughout the world to assist in recovery of disaster victims. They are life savers.

Therapy dogs are very popular with nursing homes, and some hospitals even allow them to visit. The inhabitants truly look forward to their visits. I have taken a couple of my dogs visiting and left in tears when I saw the response of the patients. They wanted and were allowed to have my dogs in their beds to hold and love.

Nationally there is a Pet Awareness Week to educate students and others about the value and basic care of our pets. Many countries take an even greater interest in their pets than Americans do. In those countries the pets are allowed to accompany their owners into restaurants and shops, etc. In the U.S. this freedom is only available to our service dogs. Even so we think very highly of the human/animal bond.

CANINE BEHAVIOR

Canine behavior problems are the number-one reason for pet owners to dispose of their dogs, either through new homes, humane shelters or euthanasia. Unfortunately there are too many owners who are unwilling to devote the necessary time to properly train their dogs. On the other hand, there are those who not only are concerned about inherited health problems but are also aware of the dog's mental stability.

You may realize that a breed and his group relatives (i.e., sporting, hounds, etc.) show tendencies to behavioral characteristics. An experienced breeder can acquaint you with his breed's personality. Unfortunately many breeds are labeled with poor temperaments when actually the breed as a whole is not affected but only a small percentage of individuals within the breed.

A pretty pair of Maltese posing politely for a holiday portrait.

If the breed in question is very popular, then of course there may be a higher number of unstable dogs. Do not label a breed good or bad. I know of absolutely awful-tempered dogs within one of our most popular, lovable breeds.

Inheritance and environment contribute to the dog's behavior. Some naïve people suggest inbreeding as the cause of bad temperaments. Inbreeding only results in poor behavior if the ancestors carry the trait. If there are excellent temperaments behind the dogs, then inbreeding will promote good temperaments in the offspring. Did you ever consider that inbreeding is what sets the characteristics of a breed? A purebred dog is the end result of inbreeding. This does not spare the mixed-breed dog from the same problems. Mixed-breed dogs frequently are the offspring of purebred dogs.

When planning a breeding, I like to observe the potential stud and his offspring in the show ring. If I see unruly behavior, I try to look into it further. I want to know if it is genetic or environmental, due to the lack of training and socialization. A good breeder will avoid breeding mentally unsound dogs.

Not too many decades ago most of our dogs led a different lifestyle than what is prevalent today. Usually mom stayed home so the dog had human companionship and someone to discipline it if needed. Not much was expected

from the dog. Today's mom works and everyone's life is at a much faster pace.

The dog may have to adjust to being a "weekend" dog. The family is gone all day during the week, and the dog is left to his own devices for entertainment. Some dogs sleep all day waiting for their family to come home and others become wigwam wreckers if given the opportunity. Crates do ensure the safety of the dog and the house. However, he could become physically and emotionally crippled if he doesn't get enough exercise and attention. We still appreciate and want the companionship of our dogs although we expect more from them. In many cases we tend to forget dogs are just that–*dogs* not human beings.

This young Maltese takes time out from making puppy mischief to pose for a pretty picture.

Dogs can be left crated during the day if time is made for them in the evenings and on the weekends. They accept their crates as their personal "houses" and seem to be content with their routine.

SOCIALIZING AND TRAINING

Many prospective puppy buyers lack experience regarding the proper socialization and training needed to develop the type of pet we all desire. In the first 18 months, training does take some work. Trust me, it is easier to start proper training before there is a problem that needs to be corrected.

The initial work begins with the breeder. The breeder should start socializing the puppy at five to six weeks of age and cannot let up. Human socializing is critical up through 12 weeks of age and likewise important during the following months. The litter should be left together during the first few weeks but it is necessary to separate them by ten weeks of age. Leaving them together after that time will increase competition for litter dominance. If puppies are not socialized with people by 12 weeks of age, they will be timid in later life.

Serenade has all types of friends— big and small!

The eight- to ten-week age period is a fearful time for puppies. They need to be handled very gently around children and adults. There should be no harsh discipline during this time. Starting at 14 weeks of age, the puppy begins the juvenile period, which ends when he reaches sexual maturity around six to 14 months of age. During the juvenile period he needs to be introduced to strangers (adults, children and other dogs) on the home property. At sexual maturity he will begin to bark at strangers and become more protective. Males start to lift their legs to urinate but if you desire you can inhibit this behavior by walking your boy on leash away from trees, shrubs, fences, etc.

Perhaps you are thinking about an older puppy. You need to inquire about the puppy's social experience. If he has lived in a kennel, he may have a hard time adjusting to people and environmental stimuli. Assuming he has had a good social upbringing, there are advantages to an older puppy.

Interacting with his littermates educates a pup about pack order. By observing a litter, you can pick out which pups make the rules and which ones are more submissive.

Training includes puppy kindergarten and a minimum of one to two basic training classes. During these classes you will learn how to dominate your youngster. This is especially important if you own a large breed of dog. It is somewhat harder, if not nearly impossible, for some owners to be the Alpha figure when their dog towers over them. You will be taught how to properly restrain your dog. This concept is important. Again it puts you in the Alpha position. All dogs need to be restrained many times during their lives. Believe it or not, some of the worst offenders are the eight-week-old puppies. They need to be

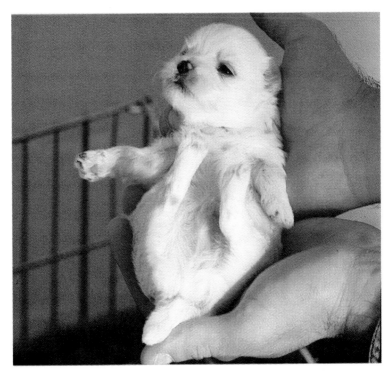

Very young puppies should only be handled by their breeder until they are properly vaccinated. gently restrained for a nail trim but the way they carry on you would think we were killing them. In comparison, their vaccination is a "piece of cake." When we ask dogs to do something that is not agreeable to them, then their worst comes out. Life will be easier for your dog if you expose him at a young age to the necessities of life—proper behavior and restraint.

UNDERSTANDING THE DOG'S LANGUAGE

Most authorities agree that the dog is a descendent of the wolf. The dog and wolf have similar traits. For instance both are pack oriented and prefer not to be isolated for long periods of time. Another characteristic is that the dog, like the wolf, looks to the leader—Alpha—for direction. Both the wolf and the dog communicate through body language, not only within their pack but with outsiders.

Every pack has an Alpha figure. The dog looks to you, or should look to you, to be that leader. If your dog doesn't receive the proper training and guidance, he very well may replace you as Alpha. This would be a serious problem and is certainly a disservice to your dog.

Eye contact is one way the Alpha wolf keeps order within his pack. You are Alpha so you must establish eye contact with your puppy. Obviously your puppy will have to look at you. Practice eye contact even if you need to hold his head for five to ten seconds at a time. You can give him a treat as a reward. Make sure your eye contact is gentle and not threatening. Later, if he has been naughty, it is permissible to give him a long, penetrating look. I caution you there are some older dogs that never learned eye contact as puppies and cannot accept eye contact. You should avoid eye contact with these dogs since they feel threatened and will retaliate as such.

BODY LANGUAGE

The play bow, when the forequarters are down and the hindquarters are elevated, is an invitation to play. Puppies play fight, which helps them learn the acceptable limits of biting. This is necessary for later in their lives. Nevertheless, an owner may be falsely reassured by the playful nature of his dog's aggression. Playful aggression toward another dog or human may be an indication of serious aggression in the future. Owners should never play fight or play tug-of-war with any dog that is inclined to be dominant.

Signs of submission are:

1. Avoids eye contact.
2. Active submission—the dog crouches down, ears back and the tail is lowered.
3. Passive submission—the dog rolls on his side with his hindlegs in the air and frequently urinates.

Signs of dominance are:

1. Makes eye contact.
2. Stands with ears up, tail up and the hair raised on his neck.
3. Shows dominance over another dog by standing at right angles over it.

Dominant dogs tend to behave in characteristic ways such as:

1. The dog may be unwilling to move from his place (i.e.,

reluctant to give up the sofa if the owner wants to sit there).

2. He may not part with toys or objects in his mouth and may show possessiveness with his food bowl.

3. He may not respond quickly to commands.

4. He may be disagreeable for grooming and dislikes to be petted.

Dogs are popular because of their sociable nature. Those that have contact with humans during the first 12 weeks of life regard them as a member of their own species–their pack. All dogs have the potential for both dominant and submissive behavior. Only through experience and training do they learn to whom it is appropriate to show which behavior. Not all dogs are concerned with dominance but owners need to be

Serenade loves to show off her beautiful flowing locks...and she wouldn't mind a tummy rub, either.

aware of that potential. It is wise for the owner to establish his dominance early on.

A human can express dominance or submission toward a dog in the following ways:

1. Meeting the dog's gaze signals dominance. Averting the gaze signals submission. If the dog growls or threatens, averting the gaze is the first avoiding action to take—it may prevent attack. It is important to establish eye contact in the puppy. The older dog that has not been exposed to eye contact may see it as a threat and will not be willing to submit.

2. Being taller than the dog signals dominance; being lower signals submission. This is why, when attempting to make friends with a strange dog or catch the runaway, one should kneel down to his level. Some owners see their dogs become dominant when allowed on the furniture or on the bed. Then he is at the owner's level.

3. An owner can gain dominance by ignoring all the dog's social initiatives. The owner pays attention to the dog only when he obeys a command.

No dog should be allowed to achieve dominant status over any adult or child. Ways of preventing are as follows:

1. Handle the puppy gently, especially during the three- to four-month period.

2. Let the children and adults handfeed him and teach him to take food without lunging or grabbing.

3. Do not allow him to chase children or joggers.

4. Do not allow him to jump on people or mount their legs. Even females may be inclined to mount. It is not only a male habit.

5. Do not allow him to growl for any reason.

Surprise! A Maltese makes a lovely gift, but introducing a dog into a new household amidst the excitement of the holidays can be overwhelming and frightening for the dog.

Not only is this Maltese a true basketball fan, it looks like he's dressed and ready to take to the court himself! Bred and owned by Sandra Kenner and Chris Pearson.

6. Don't participate in wrestling or tug-of-war games.

7. Don't physically punish puppies for aggressive behavior. Restrain him from repeating the infraction and teach an alternative behavior. Dogs should earn everything they receive from their owners. This would include sitting to receive petting or treats, sitting before going out the door and sitting to receive the collar and leash. These types of exercises reinforce the owner's dominance.

Young children should never be left alone with a dog. It is important that children learn some basic obedience commands so they have some control over the dog. They will gain the respect of their dog.

FEAR

One of the most common problems dogs experience is being fearful. Some dogs are more afraid than others. On the lesser side, which is sometimes humorous to watch, my dog

151

can be afraid of a strange object. He acts silly when something is out of place in the house. I call his problem perceptive intelligence. He realizes the abnormal within his known environment. He does not react the same way in strange environments since he does not know what is normal.

On the more serious side is a fear of people. This can result in backing off, seeking his own space and saying "leave me alone" or it can result in an aggressive behavior that may lead to challenging the person. Respect that the dog wants to be left alone and give him time to come forward. If you approach the cornered dog, he may resort to snapping. If you leave him alone, he may decide to come forward, which should be rewarded with a treat.

Vicki's daughter Tara has grown up with Maltese, and she still loves the breed now as much as she did in childhood.

Some dogs may initially be too fearful to take treats. In these cases it is helpful to make sure the dog hasn't eaten for about 24 hours. Being a little hungry encourages him to accept the treats, especially if they are of the "gourmet" variety. I have a dog that worries about strangers since people seldom stop by my house. Over the years she has learned a cue and jumps up quickly to visit anyone sitting on the sofa. She learned by herself that all guests on the sofa were to be trusted friends. I think she felt more comfortable with them being at her level, rather than towering over her.

Dogs can be afraid of numerous things, including loud noises and thunderstorms. Invariably the owner rewards (by comforting) the dog when it shows signs of fearfulness. I had a terrible problem with my favorite dog in the Utility obedience class. Not only was he intimidated in the class but he was afraid of noise and afraid of displeasing me. Frequently he would knock down the bar jump, which clattered dreadfully. I gave him credit because he continued to try to clear it, although he was terribly scared. I finally learned to "reward" him every time he knocked down the jump. I would jump up and down, clap my hands and tell him how great he was. My psychology worked, he relaxed and eventually cleared the jump with ease. When your dog is frightened, direct his attention to something else and act happy. Don't dwell on his fright.

AGGRESSION

Some different types of aggression are: predatory, defensive, dominance, possessive, protective, fear induced, noise provoked, "rage" syndrome (unprovoked aggression), maternal and aggression directed toward other dogs. Aggression is the most common behavioral problem encountered. Protective breeds are expected to be more aggressive than others but with the proper upbringing they can make very dependable companions. You need to be able to read your dog.

Many factors contribute to aggression including genetics and environment. An improper environment, which may include the living conditions, lack of social life, excessive punishment, being attacked or frightened by an aggressive dog, etc., can all influence a dog's behavior. Even spoiling him and giving too much praise may be detrimental. Isolation and the lack of human contact or exposure to frequent teasing by children or adults also can ruin a good dog.

Human contact, gentle handling, and socialization from an early age will help your Maltese puppy grow up to be well adjusted and will help prevent him from becoming fearful.

Lack of direction, fear, or confusion lead to aggression in those dogs that are so inclined. Any obedience exercise, even the sit and down, can direct the dog and overcome fear and/or confusion. Every dog should learn these commands as a youngster, and there should be periodic reinforcement.

When a dog is showing signs of aggression, you should speak calmly (no screaming or hysterics) and firmly give a command that he understands, such as the sit. As soon as your dog obeys, you have assumed your dominant position. Aggression presents a problem because there may be danger to others. Sometimes it is an emotional issue. Owners may consciously or unconsciously encourage their dog's aggression. Other owners

Scrapper fits right in with this crowd—it's easy to see why the Maltese is classified as a toy breed!

show responsibility by accepting the problem and taking measures to keep it under control. The owner is responsible for his dog's actions, and it is not wise to take a chance on someone being bitten, especially a child. Euthanasia is the solution for some owners and in severe cases this may be the best choice. However, few dogs are that dangerous and very few are that much of a threat to their owners. If caution is exercised and professional help is gained early on, then I surmise most cases can be controlled.

More than just a lap dog, the Maltese is popular as a pet because he is highly trainable and makes a great companion.

Some authorities recommend feeding a lower protein (less than 20 percent) diet. They believe this can aid in reducing aggression. If the dog loses weight, then vegetable oil can be added. Veterinarians and behaviorists are having some success with pharmacology. In many cases treatment is possible and can improve the situation.

If you have done everything according to "the book" regarding training and socializing and are still having a behavior problem, don't procrastinate. It is important that the problem gets attention before it is out of hand. It is estimated that 20 percent of a veterinarian's time may be devoted to dealing with problems before they become so intolerable that the dog is separated from its home and owner. If your veterinarian isn't able to help, he should refer you to a behaviorist.

PUNISHMENT

A puppy should learn that correction is sometimes necessary and should not question your authority. An older dog that has never received correction may retaliate. In my opinion there will be a time for physical punishment

If you want a lot of personality in a little dog, look no further than the Maltese. This breed is living proof that good things come in small packages.

but this does not mean hitting the dog. Do not use newspapers, fly swatters, etc. One type of correction, that is used by the mother dog when she corrects her puppies, is to take the puppy by the scruff and shake him *gently*. For the older, larger dog you can grab the scruff, one hand on each side of his neck, and lift his legs off the ground. This is effective since dogs feel intimidated when their feet are off the ground. Timing is of the utmost importance when punishment is necessary. Depending on the degree of fault, you might want to reinforce punishment by ignoring your dog for 15 to 20 minutes. Whatever you do, do not overdo corrections or they will lose value.

My most important advice to you is to be aware of your dog's actions. Even so, remember dogs are dogs and will behave as such even though we might like them to be perfect little people. You and your dog will become neurotic if you worry about every little indiscretion. When there is reason for concern—don't waste time. Seek guidance. Dogs are meant to be loved and enjoyed.

Artist Ed Glazbrook has captured the essence of the Maltese in his oil and pastel portrait of one of the breed's greatest champions, Ch. Sand Island Small Kraft Lite.

References:

   Manual of Canine Behavior, Valerie O'Farrell, British Small Animal Veterinary Association.

   Good Owners, Great Dogs, Brian Kilcommons, Warner Books.

SUGGESTED READING

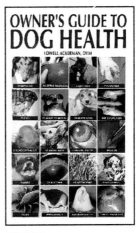

TS-214
Skin & Coat Care For
Your Dog
432 pages, over 300
full-color photos

TS-249
Owner's Guide to Dog
Health
224 pages, over 190
full-color photos

H-1067
The Book of the Maltese
256 pages, over 150
full-color photos

PS-803
The Maltese
288 pages, over 100
full-color photos

INDEX